STRESS!

HOW CHRISTIAN PARENTS COPE

Georgianna Summers

DISCIPLESHIP RESOURCES
MATERIALS FOR GROWTH IN CHRISTIAN FAITH AND LIFE

Unless otherwise indicated, all scripture is taken from the Revised Standard Version of the Holy Bible.

Library of Congress Catalog Card No. 86-71746

ISBN 0-88177-032-9

STRESS! HOW CHRISTIAN PARENTS COPE. Copyright © 1986 by Discipleship Resources. All rights reserved. Printed in the United States of America. No part of this book may be reproduced in any manner whatsoever without written permission except in the case of brief quotations embodied in critical articles or reviews. For information address Discipleship Resources Editorial Offices, P. O. Box 840, Nashville, TN 37202.

CONTENTS

1. What Is the World Coming to?   1
2. Loving Our Children—with No Strings Attached   7
3. Finding Strength We Didn't Know We Had   17
4. Putting First Our Trust in God   27
5. Learning to Heal Relationships   37
6. Coping with Illness and Death   47
7. With a Little Help from Our Community of Faith   57
8. The Good News about the Bad News   67

   Notes   73

   The Bible and Difficult Relationships   74

   Resources   75

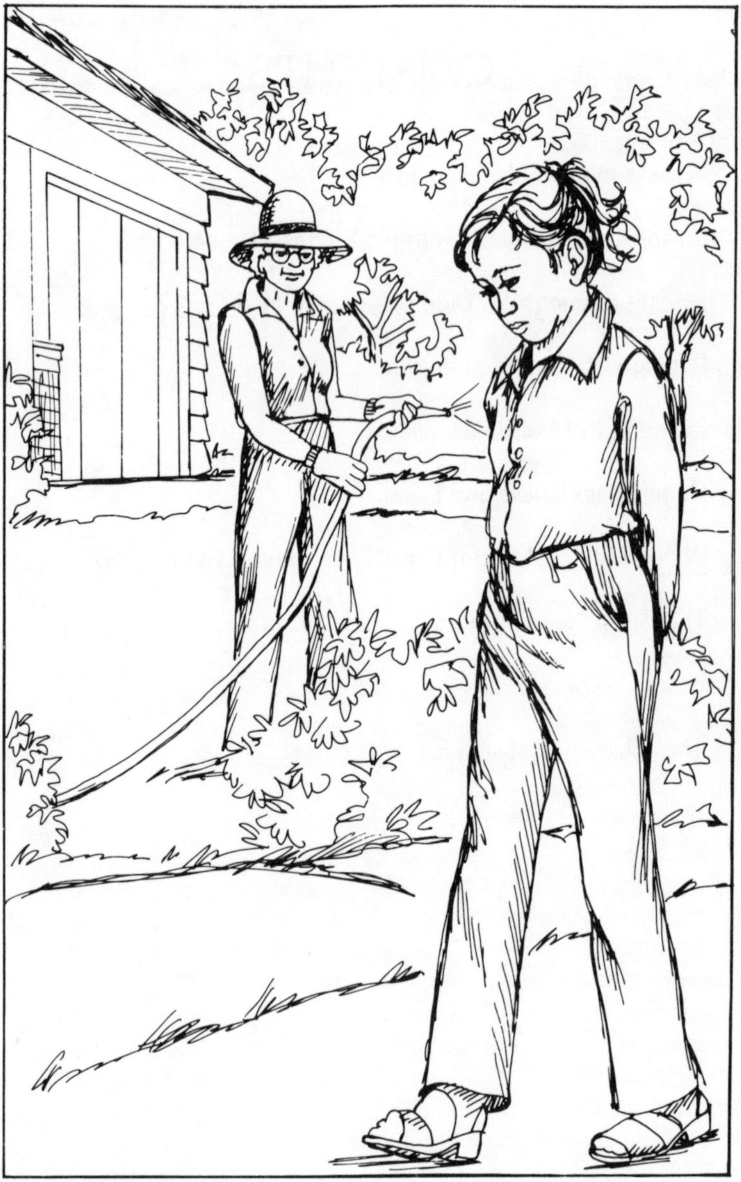

Chapter One

WHAT IS THE WORLD COMING TO?

Mrs. Martin was watering her yard when the sounds of a family squabble reached her ears.

"I hate you! You're the worst mother there ever was!"

"You take that back, young lady. You don't talk to your mother like that!"

"Let go of me, Dad. Don't touch me. I'm leaving home right now, and I'm never coming back!"

"Good heavens!" Mrs. Martin thought. "What's going on at the Davises?" Just then their front door slammed, and she saw their twelve-year-old daughter storm down the sidewalk and up the street.

"What is the world coming to?" she thought. "The Davises seem like such a nice family—civic-minded, active in their church. In my day I can't remember these kinds of things happening in good, responsible families. Why is this?"

Well, Mrs. Martin, there are lots of reasons, but one predominant cause is that we are living in a time of tremendous change. Teilhard de Chardin, the Roman Catholic paleontologist and theologian, observed that at any period of evolutionary change in the physical world, at least two characteristics are evident: Everything becomes intensified and speeded up right before the change occurs; and a lot of destruction is involved as the new emerges. It seems to me that, socially and culturally, we are living in such a time.

The structure of family life has changed. The nuclear family—mother, father, and a couple of children—is now in the minority. Single-parent families are common. Separation, divorce, unwed parents are all accepted lifestyles. For many parents this signals a change in moral values and creates conflict both within and between them and their children.

As new attitudes and lifestyles emerge in our society, the destructive effects of tension are evidenced in those who find it difficult to cope with too much change too fast. Many children, youth, and adults suffer physical ailments related to stress— hypertension, ulcers, asthma. The psychological damage is evidenced by the increase in mental illness, depression, even suicide among the young as well as adults. Society as a whole has responded and contributed to the situation by promoting consumerism, thrill-seeking, violence, drug usage, sexual promiscuity.

In the midst of this personal and social stress, what does the Christian faith have to say to parents? What do our beliefs, our personal disciplines, our churches have to offer families in times of crisis and tension? At least six affirmations:

1. God Initiates Change.

The Christian faith is not against change. From its inception in the life and teachings of Jesus, our faith has been a catalyst for change. Jesus came with new wine that could not be stored in old wineskins. His ministry was a radical example of the movement of God's Spirit in the lives of people. Moreover, when he said, "I came to set the earth on fire and how I wish it were already kindled!" (Luke 12:49, TEV), he announced his purpose as one that could cause upheaval and even family dissension.

Can it be that some of the rapid changes occurring in our time are a result of the movement of God's creative Spirit? If this is true, then to align ourselves *with* creative change instead of *against* it is part of the Christian ethic.

2. God Loves Us Unconditionally.

At the heart of our faith is a belief in a God who loves us unconditionally. We do not earn this love by our behavior, by keeping all of God's laws as the Pharisees maintained. Of course it would be ideal if we did keep God's laws all the time. However, the truth is that we all fail at times; if God loved us only when we succeeded, we would be in big trouble! But God loves us unconditionally, even when we fail.

This means that when as parents we fail to respond maturely in a crisis situation with our children, God still loves us. We don't have to beat ourselves with guilt or throw up our hands in despair. We can forgive ourselves and try again. Furthermore, we can begin to love our children unconditionally when we know that we ourselves are loved in this way by God. "We love because [God] first loved us" (1 John 4:19).

3. God Empowers Us.

Our faith affirms that we are not alone. The Christian believes that God is personally concerned about human beings and their problems. This means that when we face a crisis situation, we can draw upon a wisdom that is greater than ours and upon an enabling power to help us act out of this wisdom.

This enabling power is often what marks the difference between the religious and the secular person. Many people gain insights for coping with stress from secular experts in such fields as medicine, psychology, sociology, education. Much of this secular wisdom is valid and helpful when followed, but the difficulty for most of us is that often we are unable to follow it. Our upbringing, our overlearned responses, our emotions may prevent us from acting as we know we should.

When our children rail out against us in anger, we may yell back with damaging words. When disasters such as unemployment, illness, or death strike, we may fall apart emotionally, adding to the stress our children are also experiencing. But our faith gives us the power to respond to stressful situations creatively, following the advice of the secular experts as well as our own inner guidance. "Hence, I remind you to rekindle the gift of God that is within you . . . for God did not give us a spirit of timidity but a spirit of power and love and self-control" (2 Tim. 1:7).

4. We Have a Guideline for Setting Priorities.

The Christian faith gives us a guideline for establishing priorities. Whenever we are confronted with a crisis, the normal response is to give it first priority in our lives. However, if we continue to do this day after day, the crisis begins to rule us. Depending on the nature and length of the situation, we can be overcome with anger, anxiety, depression, fear. We are no longer in control.

Some years ago there was a television drama about a mother whose son was killed in Vietnam by "friendly" fire—that is, killed mistakenly by American artillery. She was angered by this and by the military's attitude toward it, and took on the issue as her personal cause. In a sense it helped her deal with her grief, but she became so obsessed by it that she alienated her other son and husband. It began to control her life.

The Christian faith holds firmly to Jesus' admonition to seek first God's kingdom. It puts God in the center of our lives so that we don't have to be controlled by any situation we have to face.

5. We Have Guidelines for Healing Relationships.

The Christian faith has some remarkable insights for healing relationships. Because its focus is on God and away from self, it dares to suggest such revolutionary ideas as loving our enemies, praying for those who persecute us, going the second mile, forgiving seventy times seven. Jesus' formula for healing relationships invariably involved *working with* rather than *going against*.

Today, society is trying this very approach in many areas—for example, in programs for victims and perpetrators of sexual abuse. Both victims and offenders as well as their families meet together with skilled counselors to share and discuss how each feels. The success of this type of program is verified by the healing that takes place in all those involved.

6. We Have a Support Group.

Finally, our faith offers us a support group—the fellowship of the Christian community, the church. There was a time when church people sat in judgment on those whose lives were broken by society's ills. For this reason family problems were kept hidden. The church's attitude, instead of helping to heal, often contributed to the stress that the family was facing.

Fortunately, this is no longer true. There is hardly a family in our society that has not been touched by wrenching crisis, and by at least some of the evolutionary changes of our times. The church is a community of healing, where Christian friends care for each other day and night. It offers support groups for those undergoing crisis situations, provides counseling, and shares its spiritual resources to keep alive the flame of faith and hope in those who are discouraged.

Best of all, it offers the healing power of unconditional love. Recently I heard of a small congregation that demonstrated this. A sixteen-year-old girl from a family in the congregation became pregnant, though unmarried. Church members surrounded the family and the girl with love and acceptance and went with them through the pregnancy and the birth of the child. The baby became "their" baby, the young mother a welcomed participant in the life of the church. When people find this kind of support, Paul's affirmation becomes true for them: In everything God works for good with those who love God (Rom. 8:28).

In this book we will explore how Christian parents cope with crisis and stress, using the above resources. Although we will make some use of the psychological wisdom of our time, this is not a psychology book. It is rather a look at how our Christian faith empowers us as parents and guides us in working through times of stress with our children, so that family bonds may be deepened and all family members may continue to grow.

We usually think of stress as "bad news." After all, it's not exactly pleasant. But we may discover in the pages that follow that stress can become an opportunity for good news, a door into unanticipated new possibilities for us and our children—a gift from God, if you please. At least this is my hope.

You are encouraged to read slowly, to take time to reflect on the questions scattered through each chapter, and little by little, to make some decisions about how you will accept and use the gift of stress in your family.

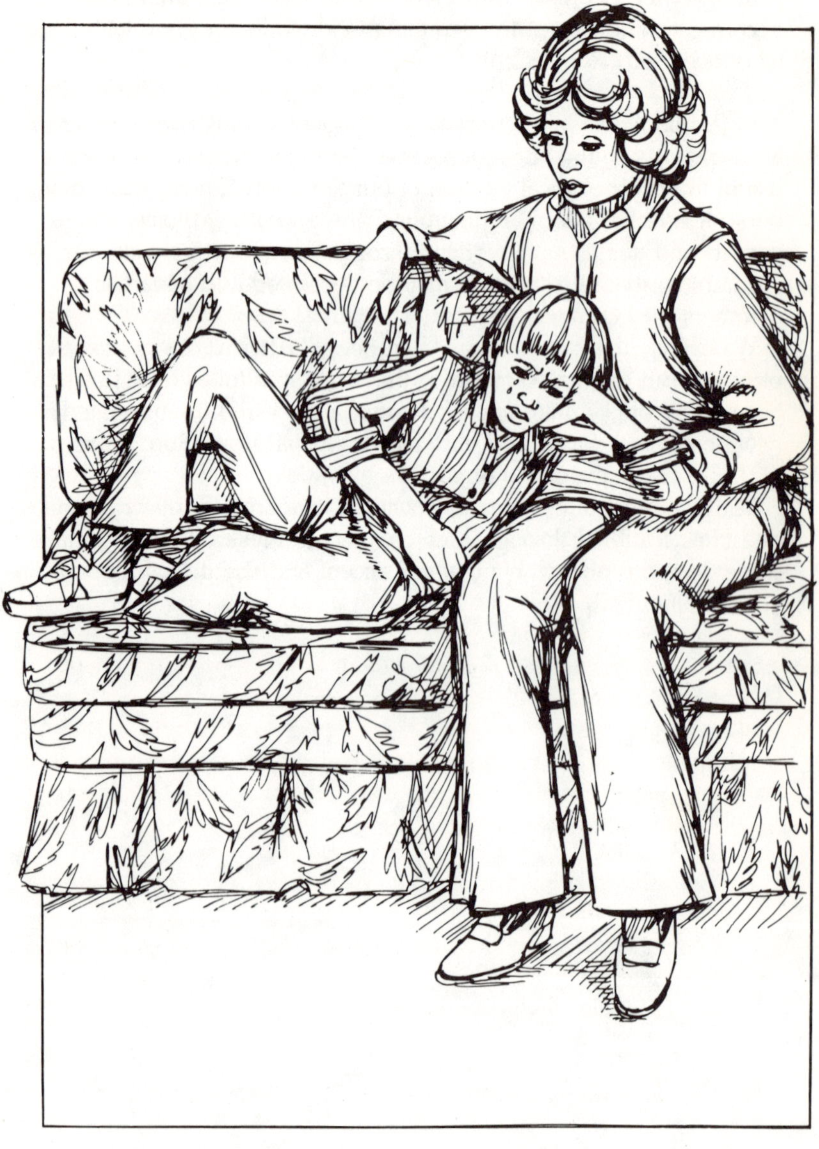

Chapter Two

LOVING OUR CHILDREN—WITH NO STRINGS ATTACHED

It was that time of year again—parent conferences at school. How Marilyn dreaded the one for Eric. She knew it was stressful for him too because of the criticisms of the teacher and the pressures that would be put on him to do better. It was the same every year: "Eric doesn't pay attention. He only does his homework halfway. He makes D's and F's on his tests."

Not only was it hard for Marilyn to face the teacher, but she couldn't face her friends either. They all had glowing reports about their children, and she hated listening to all this. It only made her feel worse about Eric and herself. Where had she failed with him? His older brother and sister were good students. Why wasn't he?

Anger welled up in her. She'd have to put more pressure on Eric to do his homework, stand over him to see that he did it right, take away his privileges if he daydreamed in school. How she hated doing this! How she hated him! No, of course not. She loved him—but if only he were different. *What could she do to change the situation?*

Most parents ask this question many times in the course of rearing children as they deal with the stresses that they and their children experience in the normal process of their growing up. We all have expectations for our children. For their sake we hope they will be healthy, bright, moral, well-liked, happy, obedient. Besides, if they are, it reflects well on us as parents. If they aren't, we feel we have to do something to change them, for their own well being, and perhaps for the sake of our own image.

> 1. *Bring to mind one of your children (or if you're not a parent, a child you know and love). Can you name a few behaviors that seem to cause stress and which you sometimes would like to change? How are you dealing with these behaviors? How well is this working?*

1. God Loves Us Unconditionally.

What does our Christian faith have to say to us when we are concerned about the behavior or character of our children? What did

Jesus have to say about the nature of God and our relationship to our children?

Jesus affirmed that God loves each of us regardless of our behavior. "[God] makes [the] sun to shine on bad and good people alike, and gives rain to those who do good and to those who do evil" (Matt. 5:45, TEV). Furthermore, he told a parable about parenting. "There was a man who had two sons . . . " (Luke 15:11).

While traditionally we have called this the parable of the prodigal son, theologians have pointed out that it has more to do with the nature of the father. Neither son is perfect. One is irresponsible and immoral. The other one is self-righteous and unforgiving. Their behavior does not in any way affect the father's love for them. The father does not say to the younger son, "I'll love you when you have paid me back for everything you squandered. I'll forgive you when you have become what I want you to be." No. "He was still a long way from home when his father saw him; his heart was filled with pity, and he ran, threw his arms around his son, and kissed him" (Luke 15:20, TEV).

Furthermore, the father does not say to the older son, "You can come in when you've quit being judgmental and self-righteous. Stay out here until your feelings toward your brother are loving and forgiving." Instead he "came out and begged him to come in. . . . And he said, 'My son, you are always here with me, and everything I have is yours'" (Luke 15:28,31).

What does this say to us as parents? To me it says that we can love our children in the same way that God loves us—without conditions. Even young children sense their need for love, and hunger for it even as we do. This was borne out in a recent survey in which 80 percent of those polled who were under fifteen years of age said love was the most important thing parents can give their children.[1]

The problem with the word *love* is that it has been so misused and overused that it has all but lost its meaning in our society. When Jesus spoke of the love of God and the love we should have for each other, he was not speaking of some sentimental, spineless emotion, but a power both strong and winsome enough to bring good out of bad or difficult situations. He, of course, ultimately demonstrated the power of this kind of love in his own life. This is the love that our children need from us.

Many people think that unconditional love is weak because it seems to overlook wrong behavior. But in reality it is strong, for it refuses to let behavior or personality traits stand in the way of our acceptance of another. Sometimes children so desperately need to know if they are loved that they will go to great lengths to test us with "unacceptable" behavior. This kind of child is trying to find a love that cannot be dissolved or changed into hate no matter how much it is attacked.

> 2. Do you find yourself withholding love from your children until they have met certain conditions? Do you expect them to be more like you, like their siblings? To behave better? Reflect on some recent stressful situation to see if your love is, in part, conditional.
> 3. We are not God. Is unconditional love possible for us? For you? How can you move in this direction?

2. Our Love Can Enable Growth.

In the area of behavior, the concept of loving without conditions raises some valid questions for parents with high standards. Does this mean we are to accept any kind of behavior with no attempt to change it? Are we to be totally permissive parents, expecting nothing of our children and accepting anything they do?

Absolutely not! This was not Jesus' way. In the case of the woman taken in adultery, Jesus admonished her to sin no more. However, this came after his acceptance of her as a person. The same was true with Zacchaeus, who was cheating and exploiting his fellow Jews. First Jesus accepted him by saying in essence, "I want to be your friend." Having a meal with him was a visible sign of friendship. Once Zacchaeus felt loved and accepted as a person, he changed his behavior.

So often, because of our distress over a child's behavior or personality problem, we put the sermon *before* the personal acceptance. At least it seems this way to the child who senses the disapproval, hears only the criticism, and consequently feels unloved and unlovely. This can carry over into adulthood. Recently a young woman said to me, "Every time my father calls, the first thing he asks is, 'Have you lost any weight yet?' It's as though the only thing he sees about me is my weight, and this is all I see about myself."

A low self-image leads to hopelessness. Imagine how hopeless both the adulterous woman and Zacchaeus must have felt about themselves. They saw no possibility or reason to change until Jesus communicated his love and acceptance of them without criticism or condemnation.

"How can *we* do this?" After all, we aren't Jesus. Besides that, he was dealing with casual relationships, not with someone he had to live with day after day. Also he wasn't emotionally involved with these people. He didn't have a vested interest in them as we do with our children for whose future we have an overwhelming concern.

All of this is true, but the principle of unconditional love which he demonstrated by his actions and his life is still valid. Furthermore, there are some spiritual disciplines that, if followed, can enable us to grow in this basic Christian principle as we relate to each other in our families.

> 4. *How do you balance your disapproval of certain behaviors with your love for the child—especially when your own feelings are involved? Evaluate how well you managed to provide correction with love in a recent situation.*

3. We Can Open Ourselves to God's Love.

In the stress of raising children, it is essential for parents to take time to be alone and quiet. During this quiet time it is often better simply to listen to God, rather than to pour out all our needs and try to tell God what to do. To be quiet and sense God's love and presence helps us to know that we ourselves are loved without condition.

A mother relates this true incident. When her oldest son was about five, her aunt came to visit from out of state. Her younger son was still a baby, and the aunt lavished lots of attention and affection on him during her two-week stay. When she left, the five-year-old spent the day misbehaving. Finally it occurred to the mother what the problem was. She asked the child if he felt she loved his little brother more than him, and his response was, "Mommy, my love tank is all empty."

As parents we need to have our love tanks filled if we are going to have a supply to give to our children. We can and do receive love from other people; but we also need to receive a daily supply from the primary source, which is God. The writer of First John knew this when he affirmed that we are able to love because God first loved us (4:19).

Sometimes we are so weary from living with stress that it is impossible to pray or even to sense the presence of God. I recall one such time when I arose before dawn too upset to sleep or to pray. I sat in the pre-dawn darkness crying, and in the silence the word *Abide* came to me. With it came a peace, an inner knowledge that there was a sustaining power in which I could rest. I was not being held accountable for my failure as a parent or condemned for my anger at the child who was causing me so much pain. My human frailties were understood, and I was loved.

Then the words of George Matheson's magnificent hymn-poem began to sing in my head:

> O Love that wilt not let me go,
> I rest my weary soul in thee;
> I give thee back the life I owe,
> That in thine ocean depths its flow
> May richer, fuller be.[2]

My anger began to melt and my pain to abate; and even though I knew the situation would still be unchanged with the day, I found I was able to love.

> 5. *What times of prayer have you found useful in restoring your capacity to love? What new approach would you like to try?*

4. We Can Let Go of Judgments.

In her book, *Something More,* Catherine Marshall shares the struggle she had in loving and forgiving her stepdaughter who was doing some unlovable things. She points out the importance of letting go of our judgments with the insight that by our judgment of others we may well bind them to the very kind of behavior we want to free them from.[3]

While it isn't easy to let go of judgments, she suggests that we can "set the rudder of our will" in that direction. I like that image. The set of the rudder determines the direction a boat will go. It is a spiritual discipline to will an action or attitude. We are the only ones who can do this, but once the rudder is set, God can provide the wind of the Spirit to move us in that direction.

Jesus has some things to say about judgments in the Sermon on the Mount (Matt. 7:1-5). His illustration of the log in our own eye and the speck in our brother's is a reminder that as parents we are not perfect either. For example, we may be discouraged over a child who is continually in trouble at home and school because she won't obey. "Won't she ever learn?" we moan in despair. If we are honest, isn't there some habit or behavior— impatience or anger or procrastination—that continues to plague *us?* Such honest appraisal of ourselves may help us to be more understanding and forgiving of our children.

In releasing our judgments of another we find that we are able to appreciate and give thanks for the whole person, even though we may not "like" every attribute. The image of a dark and light striped rubber ball comes to mind. The dark stripes are the attributes we dislike, but if we cut them out, we will destroy the ball. They are as much a part of the ball as the light areas. They give it pattern; they make it unique. All the stripes, both light and dark, make up the whole ball.

With this image in mind, we can see our children as whole persons and thank God for everything that makes up their personalities. "Thank you, God, for Michael's energy (a light stripe); thank you for his stubbornness (a dark stripe); thank you for his athletic ability (a light stripe); thank you for his procrastination (a dark stripe)."

With this kind of exercise we can begin to see Michael not as a hopeless, stubborn procrastinator, but as a unique, interesting individual. Our image of him changes. We see him differently, and consequently, he sees himself differently. Because he no longer sees himself as hopeless, he may even decide he can change. Also we may decide he doesn't need to change some of those traits that we had judged to be dark or unacceptable. Thanking God for the whole person is another way to love without conditions.

> 6. *Are you harboring some judgments of a child that tend to limit your love? How can you release these? How can you give thanks for the whole child?*

5. We Can Project Positive Images.

Once we can let go of judgments and see a child as a unique individual with a variety of traits, we need to project this positive image so she or he can see it also.

When children think poorly of themselves, it is as though they were looking at a screen on which is projected an ugly or distorted image. They see themselves in this way, and so do others. It is the Christian's belief that this is not the way God sees us. God sees our unique gifts and what we can become by developing them. If we parents can project this kind of image to our children, they will tend to grow in that direction.

Jesus did this with Simon Peter. In this case he was not dealing with a casual acquaintance but with a close friend in whom he had invested his hopes and dreams for the continuation of his ministry. He had much the same concern for Simon as parents do for their children.

One of Simon's light stripes was his enthusiasm and eagerness. Next to it was his dark stripe of not following through on his commitments. In other words, you could depend on Simon to be undependable. Not a likely prospect for a church foundation.

Jesus, however, saw a quality of strength there and projected to him the image of a person who could be firm and dependable. He did this by giving him a new name—*Peter*, which means "rock." "I tell you, you are Peter, and on this rock I will build my church, and the powers of death shall not prevail against it" (Matt. 16:18). Of course, Peter did not always live up to this image. But Jesus saw this quality in him and affirmed it, and Peter did indeed become one of the foundations of the early church.

How can we do this with our children? First we need to erase our own judgments about what qualities are better than others. We may feel it's more important to be gifted in math than in music, or to be athletic than studious. Naturally, it would be wonderful to have children who were outstanding in everything, but few are. Children quickly sense if we don't value the gifts they have as much as the ones we wished they had. In truth, all gifts are needed; all are equally valued by God. Paul grasped this when he compared the gifts of church members with the parts of the human body, pointing out it is God's Spirit that is the giver of all gifts (1 Cor. 12).

Second, if we want to see certain less obvious qualities developed in our children, we must first project to them their obvious strengths. Then when they feel good about what they know they can do or be, they themselves will have the motivation and strength to work on their weaker areas. When the desire to grow in a certain area becomes theirs and not just ours, we as parents can then lend our support to help them succeed. What a joy it is, for instance, to help a child with schoolwork when the child wants to learn and welcomes our help. It then becomes a shared experience rather than a get-off-my-back struggle.

When projecting a child's gifts it is important to hold up what is really there and not what we want to be there. Children are not easily fooled. To tell a boy he has mechanical ability when in fact he is "all thumbs" may serve only to frustrate him and make him feel even more inadequate as he tries desperately to live up to his parents' expectations.

However, often children are not able to see what is there. For instance, a child who reluctantly gives an oral report at school may see herself as timid and fearful but in reality may have more courage than those for whom standing in front of a group is easy. This can be pointed out and affirmed. "I'm proud of you for having the courage to make that report today." The child then can say to herself, "Yeah, I guess I really was pretty brave to do that."

If we see qualities in our children that are hidden to them, not only can we point these out, but we can act as enablers to help bring them out. If we simply affirm that they are there, they may not believe us, but if we work with them so they can experience the quality or ability themselves, then they will see that the image we have projected of them as true.

Recently I heard a speaker say there are four songs a person must be able to sing to be a whole person, and they must be in this order: "I am important. I am adequate. I am loved. I can love." A mother once asked me, "How can you convince a child that you love him? My son keeps asking me over and over, Do you love me, Mommy?' No matter how much I assure him that I do, he won't believe me." I suspect the boy may have not yet been able to sing, "I am adequate," and so could not accept her love because he did not feel good about himself.

Those of us who have experienced the devastation of feeling inadequate know that no amount of assurance that we are loved and accepted can compensate for the inner feeling that we have failed. Therefore it is important to act as enablers for our children so they can experience their own strengths and sing, "I am adequate." Then they will be able to accept love from others and from God, and because they know they are loved they will be able to love others as they love themselves.

7. *Consider an area of recent stress in your family. How could the projection of a more positive image have helped? What image? How could this be done?*

8. *How can you help your children feel more adequate, feel really good about themselves?*

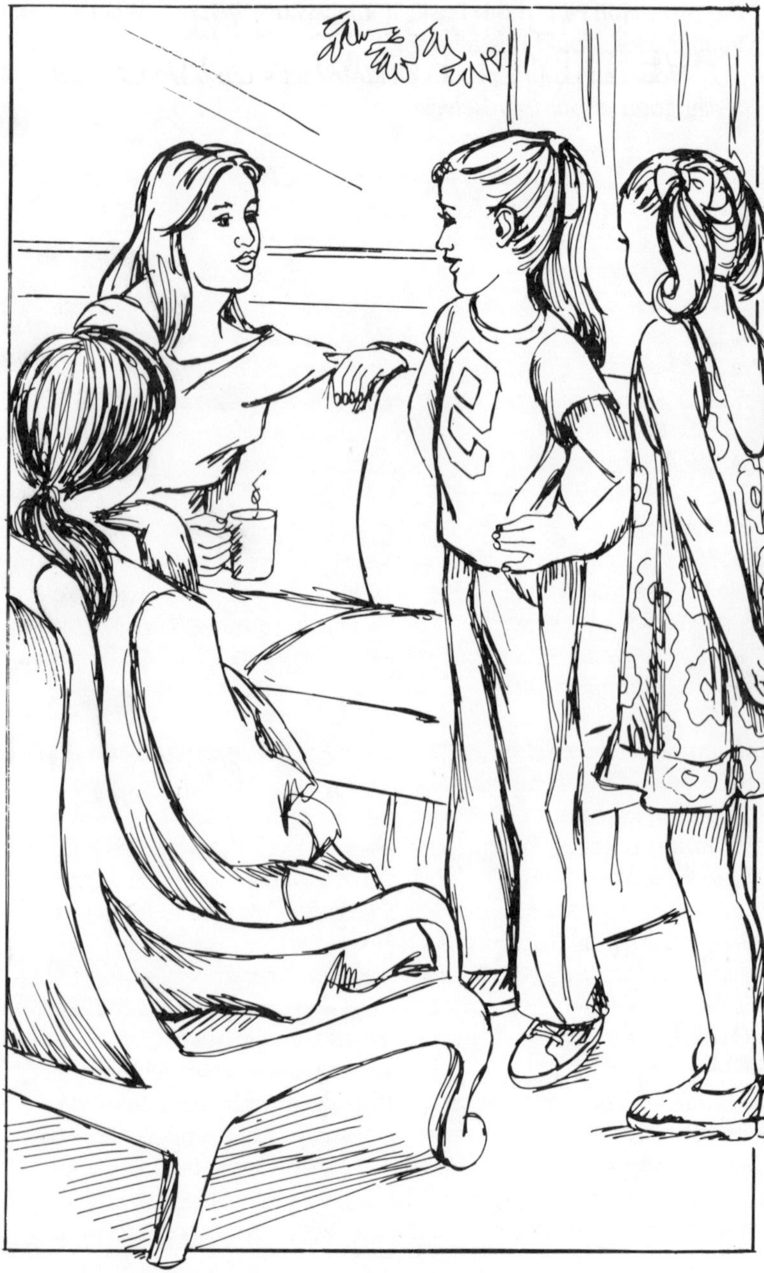

Chapter Three
FINDING STRENGTH WE DIDN'T KNOW WE HAD

Carol and Sue were visiting at Sue's house. Their ten-year-old daughters, Shawn and Kim, interrupted their conversation. "Can we go up to the shopping center, Mom?" Shawn asked Carol.

"Oh no!" Carol thought. "Not again." She didn't like Shawn to hang out at the shopping center after school. There were older kids there. She had heard it was a place for buying and selling drugs. There was so much shoplifting these days too. Still it could be a harmless request. She'd be with Kim, and Kim was a responsible child. If she said no, there would be a scene. Shawn always made fun of her objections, and ended up accusing, "You don't trust me."

"Can we go, Mom?" Kim asked Sue.

Sue answered calmly, "You know the answer, Kim. We've already discussed what goes on up there. I'm sure you girls can find something interesting to do here."

"But Mom!" Kim protested. "There's nothing to do. We're bored."

"Come on, Mom," Shawn wheedled. "There's nothing wrong with going to the shopping center. All our friends are there. Don't you trust us?"

Sue answered again. "It's not a good place for you girls to be after school, Shawn. Kim is not allowed to go."

The girls went back to Kim's room, sullen and protesting. Carol heard Shawn mutter, "Your mom's weird."

"How do you do it, Sue?" Carol asked in admiration. "How can you be so firm and unmoved by their protests? You don't even seem bothered by their insults."

"This one was easy," Sue remarked wryly, "because Kim and I had already discussed it and agreed on a decision. If they come out again with a new request, I may not be so sure of myself."

All of us would like to meet unsettling situations with calmness and self-assurance. When we are sure of ourselves and the rightness of our decisions, we operate out of a position of inner strength. This not only averts stress for us, but it gives our children a sense of security even if they are objecting or rebelling. Our children especially need us to be calm and in control of ourselves when crises occur. How do we do it? How can our faith help us to function in a stressful situation from a position of inner strength and confidence?

In this chapter we will explore four Christian convictions about how God strengthens us—parents and children alike—for dealing with stress:

> God is with us.
> God works for us.
> God is a source of wisdom and guidance.
> God is an enabler.

>   1. *Are there some people whose inner strength you admire? What seems to be their secret?*

1. God Is with Us.

Our Christian faith affirms that we were created out of love and that this creating love is personal. The writer of 1 John spells out the nature of God and this personal relationship between God and people: "God is love, and he [or she] who abides in love abides in God, and God abides in him [or her]" (1 John 4:16). "See what love the Father has given us, that we should be called children of God; and so we are" (3:1).

To the Christian then, God is not just a power or force that at one time brought the world into being and then left its inhabitants to fend for themselves. Instead, we believe that God is interested in us, is concerned about us, in fact enters into every experience that we have. This is the doctrine of the incarnation that "the word became flesh and dwelt among us" (John 1:14).

This concept of a personal God who cares for us and all creation permeated Jesus' teachings: "Not [a sparrow] will fall to the ground without your Father's will. But even the hairs of your head are all numbered" (Matt. 10:29-30). Jesus spoke of a God who feeds the birds and clothes the lilies of the fields, and cares infinitely more about us (Matt. 6:26-30).

What then does this say to us when we are facing stress in parenting? It says, first of all, that we are not alone. Often we feel alone, especially if the stress has to do with conflicting values in society, as in the incident of the mother and the shopping center request. "All our friends are there." "Everybody's doing it." "Your mom's weird."

If we feel a minority position is the right one for us, we can become a "majority of one," upheld by our faith in a personal God who gives us the inner strength to stand by our convictions. Paul affirms in his letter to the Romans, "If God is for us, who is against us?" The Christian believes God *is* for us and with us.

> 2. *In what times of family stress have you felt alone, weak, vulnerable? Were you able to find strength in the knowledge of God's personal care? How can your faith that "God is with us" see you through a coming difficult time?*

2. God Works for Good.

"We know that in everything God works for good with those who love [God], who are called according to [God's] purpose" (Rom. 8:28). As Christian parents we know that in all the stresses that we and our children go through in the child-rearing years, God is working with us to bring good out of all our experiences.

The writer of the letter of James in the New Testament affirms this: "Consider yourselves fortunate when all kinds of trials come your way, for you know that when your faith succeeds in facing such trials, the result is the ability to endure" (James 1:2-3, TEV). The Revised Standard Version translates the beginning of this passage, "Count it all joy!"

Perhaps this is what Jesus was getting at in the beautitudes. The poor, the sorrowing, those persecuted for righteousness' sake are blessed when, through the eyes of faith, they can see God working for good in these difficult experiences. All of this says that the nature of God is love, that God is for us, that God wills good for us in and through all situations.

If we can affirm this good news, what a difference it can make in our parenting! Let us take, for example, this true situation that was shared with me. A young child was sent home from school for misbehavior. His mother's first response was to punish him. She sent him to his room where he proceeded to tear the posters off the wall and yell abusive language.

How could God work for good in this chaotic situation? Suddenly she recognized the boy's need for understanding rather than punishment, seeing his behavior as a result of frustration and too much pressure, not of naughtiness. She went into his room and listened to his side of the story. When he calmed down, they were then able to talk about what caused the problem.

In the interchange she saw some mistakes she had made—too many expectations, too much punishment, often inconsistent responses. Later she and her husband began to look at avenues to pursue for relieving the stress the boy was going through—take him to a doctor to check for physical causes, see the school psychologist, perhaps ask for a different teacher. As a result, growth and understanding came to all of them out of this stressful situation.

> 3. *Recall an occasion of crises or stress that seemed very dark at the time. Can you now see ways in which God was "working for good" even then? How can you remember this truth at the next time of stress?*

3. *God Is a Source of Wisdom and Guidance.*

A third principle that our belief in a personal God declares is that God is a source of wisdom and guidance. This was true for Jesus, as evidenced by the innumerable references in the Gospels to his time spent in prayer. He spoke to his disciples about the guidance of the Holy Spirit, saying, "When the Spirit of truth comes, he will guide you into all the truth" (John 16:13).

This was true also for Paul and the early Christians. The entire Book of Acts is full of references to the guidance of the Holy Spirit. The disciples asked for guidance in choosing someone to take Judas' place (Acts 1:24). "The Spirit gave Stephen such wisdom that when he spoke, they could not refute him" (Acts 6:10, TEV) Paul and Silas were directed by the Holy Spirit not to go into Asia but over to Macedonia (Acts 16:6-10).

Through waiting and listening

How do we receive this kind of wisdom and guidance? According to the New Testament, it comes primarily through prayer. Unfortunately, many people don't receive it through prayer because they spend more time talking than listening. Sometimes, too, we come to God with our minds already made up, asking for approval rather than guidance.

To "wait on the Lord" is a biblical injunction that many Americans find difficult to follow in this age of instant results. Yet it is in waiting that we come to "hear" the word of direction to guide us into wise decisions and to give us courage when a stressful situation seems to be going on forever. The ancient wisdom of the Old Testament affirms this: "They who wait for the Lord shall renew their strength, they shall mount up with wings like eagles, they shall run and not be weary, they shall walk and not faint" (Isa. 40:31).

This means that when we are in doubt about what to say or do in a situation involving our children, we would be wise to avoid too quick a response. A quick decision may be an unwise one; therefore, if there is any doubt in our minds, it is well to say, "I'll have to think about it."

How does God "speak" to us in the waiting period? There are a number of ways. Sometimes it's an insight through a thought that comes to mind. Once in a prayer group a mother shared that she had felt she should give her son more love because he didn't seem able to give or respond to love. She said, "I thought if I just kept pouring more love on him, eventually it would seep in." Then in her quiet time the thought came, "Let God decide how much love to give him. You just be the channel."

Later the boy confessed to her, "You were a burden to me. I felt guilty because of all you were doing for me." She could then see the wisdom of what she had "heard."

Through the Bible

God also speaks through the Bible. An insight may come as we are consciously looking for help in the Bible, or a verse of scripture may suddenly come to mind as we are praying or thinking about a problem.

I had such an experience several years ago after a phone call saying my mother had terminal cancer. To deal with this stressful news I took a walk in a wooded area behind our house, and as I faced my grief the words of Romans 8:28 sang in my head: "In everything God works for good with those who love God."

I thought of my mother's love for God and her lifetime of commitment and faithfulness. I reflected that Paul wrote "in everything"—not in some things, not in everything except this, but in everything. It was a promise that sustained me through the weeks ahead as I walked with my mother to the threshhold of the next life. It turned out to be one of the richest experiences of my life, with a minimum of stress.

God not only speaks through the Bible but also through other resources. With prayer we are sometimes led to read a book that deals with our concern. We may hear something in a discussion group that speaks directly to the situation for which we have been seeking wisdom. We may be guided to talk the problem over with a friend or with our pastor and find that person has an answer or an insight.

Through our feelings

Another source of God's guidance is through our own inner feelings. Parents need to be intuitive. Children often find it difficult to express their real feelings. Sometimes they don't know that they are feeling other than "bad." A parent who can sense that something is bothering a child can help relieve the stress the child is experiencing by helping him or her tell about it.

Sometimes a child is under stress and is afraid to tell about it. For example, a father was concerned about his son's sudden refusal to participate in Little League. "I'm quitting," the boy said. "I don't like baseball."

"I thought you enjoyed it," the father responded in surprise. "What don't you like about it?"

"I don't know." The boy shrugged his shoulders. "It's just boring."

Suddenly the father "knew" this wasn't the real reason. He had a feeling something had happened, something the boy was afraid of or ashamed to tell him. He talked to the coach and discovered the kids on the team were making fun of his son's ability to play, that even the coach didn't want him.

Had he not listened to his feeling he might have insisted that the boy play, compounding the stress he was under. Instead he let him know he knew his real reason for wanting to quit and that it was all right. There were other options, if he chose. Another year. Another coach. Some practice with him at home. Perhaps no Little League at all.

As children enter adolescence, parents who have learned to be sensitive to their hunches will find their inner feelings will often give them warning signals. Teenagers are less apt to share on their own because they are struggling to become independent and also because peer pressure is greater during these years. Parents who follow their inner guidance can often help their teenagers avoid making unwise choices, and this is a source of strength for young people. In teaching youth in Sunday school I have heard them say, "I could never get away with that. You just can't fool my dad." "I don't know how, but my mom always seems to know when something is bothering me."

God does speak to us through our hunches that something is not all it seems, through feelings that we should or should not do something. If a feeling is strong or persistent, we would be wise to listen to it.

> 4. Can you recall instances when you have received God's guidance through waiting and listening in prayer? Through study of the Bible or other resources? Through your own feelings?
>
> 5. Through what other sources do you experience God's guidance? Congregational worship? Study groups? Your children themselves? Your spouse? Dreams? To what two or three channels will you now give closer attention?

4. God Is an Enabler.

Paul wrote to the Philippians, "I can do all things in him who strengthens me" (Phil. 4:13). Paul, referring to someone who is weak, wrote to the Christians in Rome, "He will be upheld, for the Master is able to make him stand" (Rom. 14:4). God is an enabler. God is there with us in times of stress, supporting us, helping us and our children find the way.

Even after we have received guidance for a crisis situation or a decision we are faced with, we often find it difficult to follow it. We may know, for instance, that we need to back off from trying to toilet train our two-year-old because he isn't ready for it. Yet friends are saying, "All mine were trained at two," or a relative is pushing us with, "He's plenty old enough," and we find ourselves continuing in the same old pattern.

Usually the reason we are unable to follow what we know to be wise counsel is that we have overlearned a response by upbringing or practice and can't break the habit. We arise in the morning determined not to nag our eight-year-old about getting to school on time, but then we just can't keep quiet when he dawdles over breakfast and takes his time getting dressed. We resolve that the next time our daughter forgets her lunch or books we will not take them to school, knowing that the consequences of going without lunch or receiving the teacher's disapproval over the books will make her more responsible. However, it *is* a long day without lunch; she won't do well without her books; there *is* that errand we need to run near the school. . . .

How are we able to follow that which we feel is the right attitude or the wise course of action to take? The Christian believes that God is our enabler. This doesn't mean that we will change overnight or that we won't fail many times, especially if we are trying to break a long-standing response or feeling. It does mean we can ask for and receive help within and beyond ourselves on a daily or, if necessary, more frequent basis and know we are forgiven when we fail.

>   6. *Have you ever been quite clear about what to do in a stressful situation, but felt helpless to do it? What held you back? How might your awareness of God's enabling presence have helped?*
>   7. *How can you help your growing children to become more deeply aware of the four Christian affirmations of this chapter, to grow in inner strength, to depend on God's loving care, guidance, and power in the face of stress?*

All of us would like to see ourselves facing every stressful parenting experience with calm self-assurance and understanding. This, of course, is unrealistic, but it is not unrealistic to find through faith that there is a strength within us that becomes stronger with use. A belief in a God who enters into our experiences, guides us, enables us, and works for good in all things can strengthen this power within us to face whatever experiences life brings us and our children.

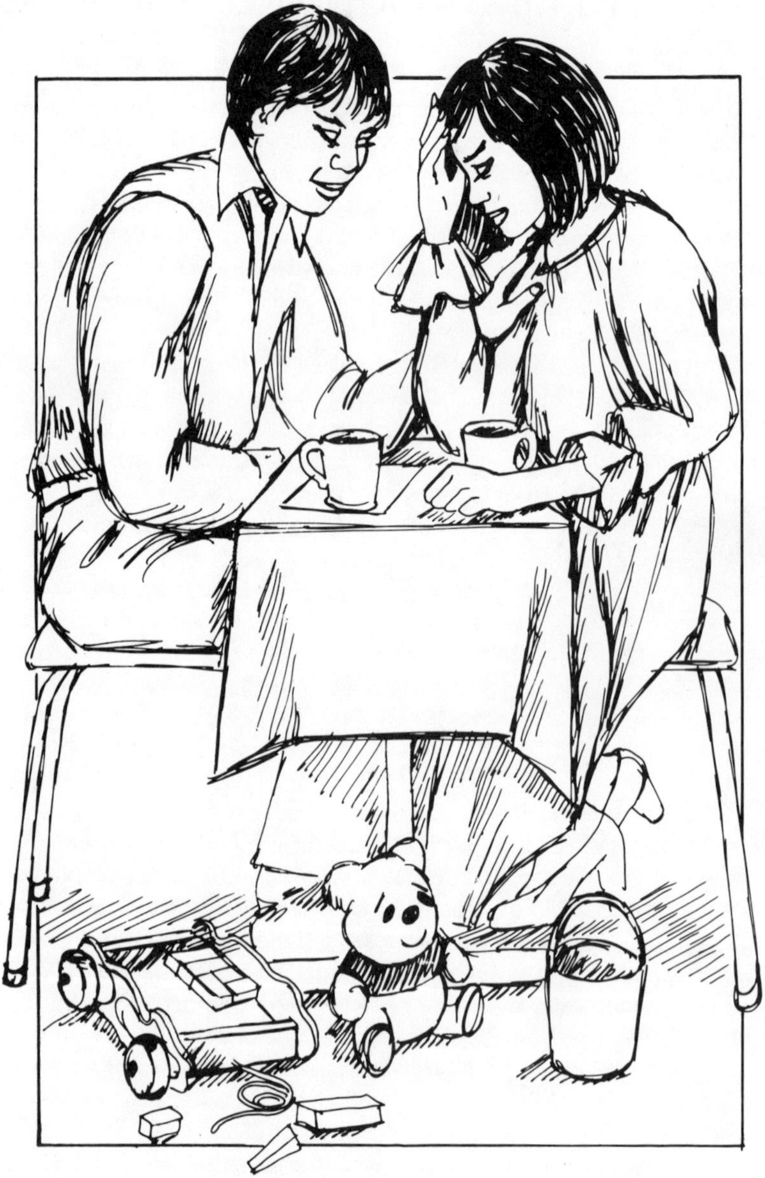

Chapter Four

PUTTING FIRST OUR TRUST IN GOD

The times were hard. Taxes were high. People could hardly eke out a living. Those who were unemployed either had to be dependent on relatives or beg for welfare from the public. Everywhere you turned someone had a hand out. What was that young man talking about? "Do not be anxious, saying, 'What shall we eat?' or 'What shall we drink?' or 'What shall we wear?' Your heavenly Father knows that you need them all. But seek first his kingdom and his righteousness, and all these things shall be yours as well" (Matt. 6:31-33).

Surveys indicate that one of the greatest causes of stress in our society today is economics. Even though we live in the world's most affluent country, young families especially are battling inflation, high interest rates which keep them from buying a home, unemployment. Often both parents have to work to pay the bills. If they work different shifts to avoid child-care expenses, they sacrifice time together as a family.

Because of the change in family structure, we have a growing number of single-parent families, 90 percent of which are headed by women. If these women work outside the home, much of their salary goes for child care, and managing a job plus the responsibilities of parenting alone adds to their stress load. Single fathers have similar problems, plus additional economic responsibility if they are paying alimony.

To say to parents in these situations, "Don't be anxious," must seem like the height of callousness. So it must have seemed to people in Jesus' day too. Women didn't usually work outside the home, but they worked from daylight to dark taking care of their families on the meager funds their husbands brought in. If they were widowed, they were dependent on family members for support of them and their children. If they were divorced, they often had no one to support them. (This is why Jesus spoke out so strongly against divorce—to protect women in a society where husbands could divorce them for no good cause.) No matter what kind of income people made, the tax collectors working for the Romans took most of it.

Economics, of course, is not the only cause of anxiety when it comes to parenting. Parents worry about their children's health and safety. In a young mother's group I asked, "What do you worry most about in raising your children?"—to which several replied, "I just worry about whether they are going to grow up at all. There are so many things that can happen to them physically."

Parents of infants and toddlers especially have this concern. There are so many things in preschoolers' environment that can harm them. Almost every parent of young children has a horror story or two. In my experience there was a gopher bite and subsequent rabies shots for an eighteen-month-old; a dash to the hospital for stomach pumping for a two-year-old. I've heard stories of pulling over a pan of hot grease, biting into a plugged-in electric cord, climbing to a dangerous height. Two-year-olds are especially adept at causing this kind of stress.

As children grow older and enter the environment of neighborhood and school, there may be another set of worries. Child molestation and kidnapping seem to be on the rise. There are drunken drivers on the loose; violence on the streets and even in the schools. Children's normal activity in games and sports brings calls from the school about broken bones, concussions, and gashed heads. Then as children enter adolescence, there's more to worry about—alcohol, drugs, and sex. "Don't be anxious." Ha!

   1. *As you think about parents you know, what worries beset them? Economics? Their children's safety? Social violence? Other dangers? How about you? What are your three most persistent worries as a parent?*

1. What Did Jesus Mean?

What did Jesus mean when he told us to trust God to take care of our needs, to seek the kingdom of God first? It might be well to understand first what he didn't mean.

He didn't mean to do nothing and let God do everything. How foolish that would be! A man who gets laid off from work isn't likely to find another job if he doesn't go out and apply for something else. A child who mistakenly takes poison may die if someone doesn't administer an antidote quickly. Drunken drivers will continue to maim and kill innocent victims unless concerned parent groups like Mothers Against Drunk Drivers fight for effective controls.

Also when Jesus said to seek the kingdom of God first he didn't mean we should spend all our time going to church, praying, or reading the Bible, to the neglect of our responsibilities as a spouse or parent. Sometimes this happens. While a mother is teaching Sunday school, serving on church committees, holding an office in the women's group, singing in the choir, and being at the church every time there's an activity, her children may be running around unsupervised or becoming resentful and bitter toward the church. Sometimes too much church activity or overzealousness for religion can drive a wedge in a marriage relationship, especially if one partner is not as interested as the other.

Worry is useless.

What did Jesus have in mind then when he said not to be anxious? One thing he was saying was that it is useless to worry. "Which of you by being anxious can add one cubit to his span of life?" (Matt. 6:27). Worry may lead to an action, but worry itself is not an action. It won't do anything but cause us stress.

Once we have child-proofed our house against the dangers that might harm a curious two-year-old, it is senseless to worry about what could happen. If we have trained our school-age children not to get into a car with strangers, to be careful in crossing a street, and to keep a distance from high-flying swings—then we have to trust that they will remember what we have taught them. We do the same with our teenagers, teaching in their pre-teen years the dangers of alcohol and drug abuse, and the serious consequences of sexual promiscuity. Then we have to trust.

It is true that our trust has sometimes been betrayed by them or other people, but worrying wouldn't have made any difference. It is so much better to live in trust than in fear, and healthier too. All the experts agree that anxiety and worry cause serious emotional and physical problems.

Worry is irreligious.

Furthermore, Jesus said that to worry is to be irreligious. When he commented that "the Gentiles seek all these things" (Matt. 6:32), he was speaking about the non-Jews who believed in pagan deities. Dr. William Barclay, renowned biblical scholar, comments, "Worry . . .

is characteristic of a heathen, and not of one who knows what God is like. Worry is essentially distrust of God. Such a distrust may be understandable in a heathen who believes in a jealous, capricious, unpredictable god; but it is beyond comprehension in one who has learned to call God by the name of Father. The Christian cannot worry because he believes in the love of God."[4]

Some years ago in the *New Yorker* there was a modern parable called "The Little Duck" written by Donald C. Babcock. In it he captured the essence of what it means to trust in God: "A duck riding the ocean a hundred feet beyond the surf . . . cuddles in the swells. . . . There is a big heaving in the Atlantic, and he is part of it. . . . He can rest while the Atlantic heaves, because he rests in the Atlantic. Probably he doesn't know how large the ocean is. And neither do you. But he realizes it. And what does he do? He sits down in it. He reposes in the immediate as if it were infinity, which it is.

"That is religion, and the duck has it. He has made himself part of the boundless by easing himself into it just where it touches him. . . . I like the little duck. He doesn't know much. But he has religion."

> 2. Recall a recent incident when you were extremely worried about a child. What part did the worry itself play in reaching a solution? How did it help? Hinder? Could you have channeled your anxiety in more constructive ways?

2. Let Us Put God First.

Jesus' antidote for worry is to put God first in our lives. This is not surprising. It comes out of his Hebrew faith. The first commandment is, "You shall have no other gods before me" (Ex. 20:3). The great commandment upon which Jesus said the whole law of Moses and the teachings of the prophets depend is, "You shall love the Lord your God with all your heart, and with all your soul, and with all your mind" (Matt. 22:37). This was the heart of his teaching and the secret of his personal life.

Setting our priorities

How does this apply to us as we cope with the stresses of parenting? It gives us a priority, shows us where to put our highest loyalty. No person deserves our total devotion. This is a good thing for parents to learn, because there *are* people who make their children their god.

In our first parish there was a young couple who had one child, a five-year-old boy. The mother literally worshiped him. He was the most important thing in her life. They discovered he had a weak heart, which required surgery to save his life. When he died on the operating table, she was totally devastated. No one—her husband, her family, her pastor—could get through to her because her god was dead. I often wondered what would have happened had the child lived and grown to adulthood. Could he have carried the heavy responsibility of being god for her? I doubt it. It's too heavy a burden for anyone.

Similarly, no stressful situation deserves our total allegiance for an extended period. It may be demanded for a brief emergency period—for example, when someone is hurt or seriously ill or dies. Most of us, however, have to live with some kind of chronic stress a great deal of the time. If we are parenting, we have to deal with personality traits in children that may cause us continual tension. We may have to cope on a daily basis with the stress of keeping up with an active two-year-old, juggle our schedules to handle all the activities of a sociable ten-year-old, or constantly assess how much freedom to give an independence-seeking teenager. If we have several children, then our chronic stress load is increased as we deal with each one's personality and age-level characteristics at the same time.

An acquaintance of mine experienced this kind of around-the-clock stress when she found her teenager was smoking marijuana. Every time her daughter left the house, panic grabbed her by the throat. Where was she going? Who was she with? What were they doing? She worried constantly while the girl was at school. She couldn't sleep if her daughter spent the night with a friend or stayed out late at a party. Finally she realized she was at the breaking point and sought help from a pastor who helped her set her priorities straight.

A sense of perspective

What happens when we focus on God instead of on a person or situation? For one thing, it gives a sense of perspective. There is more to life than this person or situation causing us stress. If we can put God first, we may even find that the things we think are most important are not.

For example, when a family is struggling to pay bills and get a little ahead financially, sometimes making money becomes a top priority. Anxiety takes over. What will happen if someone gets sick? How can we afford music lessons, orthodontics? How will we send the children to college?

Society doesn't help, with its pressures to have the "good" things in life. Both parents may feel they have to work in order to survive, or a husband may take two jobs in order to have all the material things that seem so important. When we put God first, all the other things that vie for our loyalty fall into their proper perspective, and we may even find that some of them have no importance at all.

The gift of freedom

Another benefit from putting God first is the gift of freedom. Anytime concern for a person or situation takes over our thinking for an extended period of time, we can become enslaved to the prolem. When we are burdened with worry or fear, we are not free to make wise decisions, to see beyond the present, to move through the situation with assurance. Jesus spoke to this when he said, "No one can serve two masters" (Matt. 6:24). The only one whom we should call "Master" is God, and in giving God our highest loyalty is our freedom.

On several occasions I have had the opportunity to walk with young mothers through the valley of marital difficulties heralding divorce. Consumed with the agony of rejection, they tried desperately to hang on to the relationship for the sake of the family and their own self-image. The marriage and their mate became God for them, and without them they felt they were nothing.

When they began to focus on God instead of on saving the marriage, they were able to see their way through the situation. Some were able to weather the storm and come through with a stronger relationship. Some chose or accepted divorce as the best solution. In either case they were not victims, dependent on another person for their sense of worth. Furthermore, they were able to give their children security through this difficult time without engendering anxiety and bitterness in them.

3. To what things in your life do you give top priority? What people? Where does God stand among your priorities?

4. Perhaps you have had the experience, in a time of stress, to shift your focus from the problem or the person in difficulty to God. If so, what were the results?

3. How Can We Put God First?

It is all very well to speak of the value of seeking first the kingdom of God. The real stickler is how does one do it? It is again an act of the will. We are the only ones who can make this decision and stick to it. Sometimes if the problem is all-consuming, we may have to do it on an hourly basis, disciplining ourselves to think consciously the word *God* or the phrase, *Seek first the kingdom,* whenever the problem begins to dominate our thinking.

Another way to put God first is to remember the past. All of us have come through crises and difficult times in our lives. If we are persons of faith, we recognize we have been carried through; we have been upheld and sustained by the grace of God. If this has been true in the past, it is also true in the present. A pastor was visiting with a mother and father who were experiencing a family crisis. One of their children had just had surgery for a brain tumor. Another child had been diagnosed as diabetic. The young father said, "I don't know if I can survive all this." The pastor responded quietly, "You have so far, haven't you?"

Remembering how we have been sustained through crises in the past leads to praise, which is another way to focus on God. There are so many things to be thankful for—the way our material needs are met, the times we thought we couldn't go on and did, the love that comes to us through family and friends. There is truth and wisdom in the words of the old hymn: "Count your blessings, name them one by one, and it will surprise you what the Lord has done."

Seeking God through prayer

Praise is a form of praying which brings us to the most effective way of seeking first the kingdom of God. I am speaking here of the most mature kind of prayer in which we seek God for God's sake and not for what we can get from God.

It was Jesus' faith that God knows our needs and will supply them. "Your father knows what you need before you ask him" (Matt. 6:8). Pounding on the door of heaven and pleading with God to give us what we need makes God some kind of hard-hearted tyrant, worse than we human parents who certainly would not turn a deaf ear to our children's needs. Yet it is the "give-me" prayer that we are most apt to use in a time of anxiety and stress, and if we don't get what we ask for, we may feel it does no good to pray.

One of the main reasons we often don't get what we ask for is that we ask for what we want rather than what we need. As parents we are familiar with this kind of request. Our children want only dessert for supper; they need a well-balanced meal. Our son wants us to give him a new bicycle; he needs to earn part of the money for it himself. Our daughter wants a television set of her own; she needs to learn how to share with the family. As persons older and wiser than our children, we know this. We say no out of love and concern for their physical or spiritual growth, not out of meanness or indifference.

It is easy to see this from a parent's perspective; it is more difficult when we (like a child) are praying to a heavenly parent, and seem to receive a negative response. It is especially difficult to understand when we feel that our requests are not selfish or materialistic. When a child is sick or in trouble or is behaving in unacceptable ways, we pray passionately for healing or for a change in the situation or behavior. Surely these are legitimate needs, not just wants.

Perhaps they are, but we do not have God's perspective. I know personally that I have prayed long and hard sometimes for a desire that I thought was a need only to find eventually that it was a want. God's concern is for us to grow into wholeness. What areas in our life need healing or strengthening? Are we weak in patience? Is manipulation of others a controlling force in our life? Do we need to grow in courage or trust or sensitivity? While we may want our children not to try our patience, our need may be for us to learn patience. Children who refuse to let us manipulate them may be God's way of helping us be freed from this destructive trait.

To "seek first the kingdom" then enables us to be one with God's purpose and will for our lives and the lives of our children. It helps us to clarify our needs rather than our wants. This usually does not happen immediately, and this is why Jesus said we should continue asking. It is not because God doesn't hear or has to be persuaded, but because *we* don't hear. As we continue to pray and listen, we often begin to understand what we should pray for.

The key word, of course, is *need*. The Christian believes that no matter what the circumstance and how it has come about, we can trust God to supply our need, whether it be economic, physical, emotional, or spiritual. Thus, trusting God is the most effective relief for worry in any of these areas. Putting God first in our lives will help us get our priorities in order, will give us a sense of perspective, and will help free us from the burden of anxiety so that we can move through, or live with, those situations that cause us stress.

> 5. *"Putting God first" is easy to say, difficult to do. Take some time to reflect on the meaning of this chapter for your life. For your parenting. What priorities do you really want to have? What steps will you now take in this direction?*

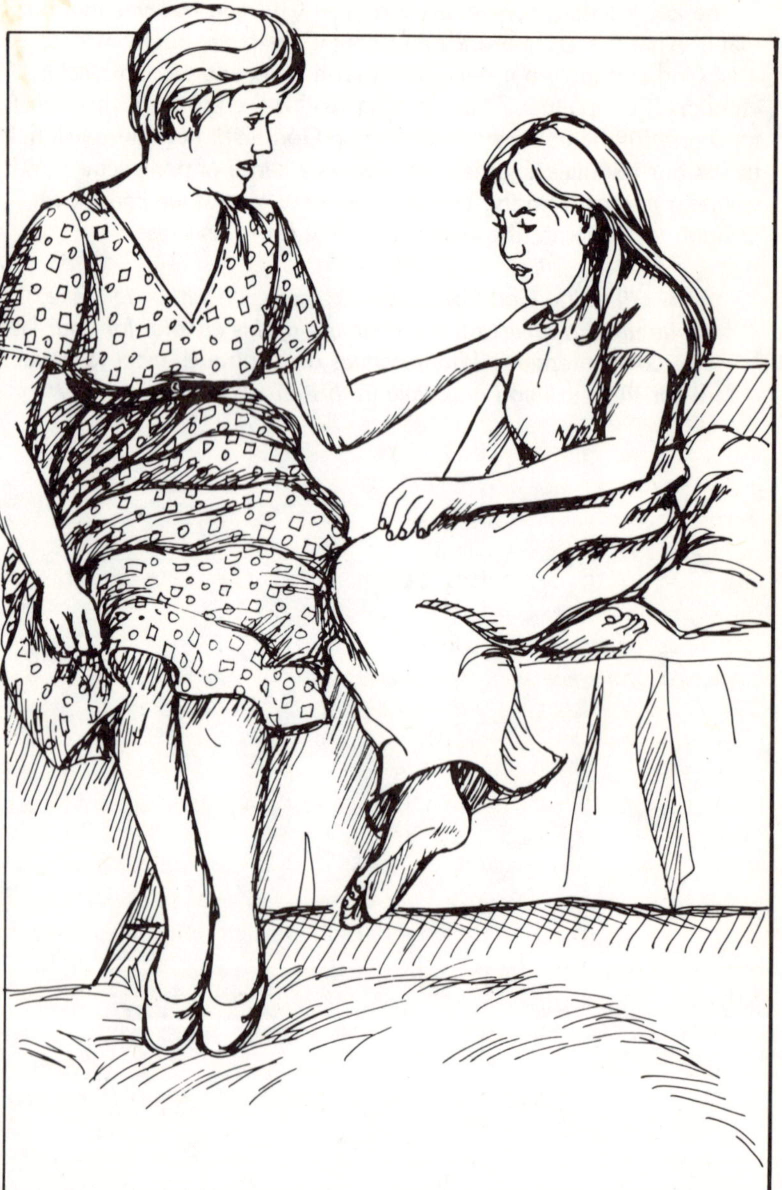

Chapter Five
LEARNING TO HEAL RELATIONSHIPS

One of the main causes of stress for most of us is the struggle to maintain harmonious relationships among those with whom we live. Living in close proximity with others causes friction, and today we are living in an increasingly crowded world.

It is not only our schedules that are crowded but our physical bodies as well. Our houses are built close together; many of us live in apartments, condominiums, high-rise complexes. When we have free time, we flock to beaches and parks to get away from it all— yet even here there is no space. Some friends of ours wanted to go camping on a holiday weekend to get away from the pressures of work and get close to nature. They drove several hundred miles trying to find a campground with a vacancy and finally ended up coming home in order to get away from all that human nature!

Home *should* be a sanctuary, yet often it is not. A mother who has been cooped up with young children all day may have reached her limit and have the need to turn over her parenting responsibilities to the returning father. The father, on the other hand, may have been under pressure at work and want only to be left alone. School-age children may want to unload the experiences of their day or retreat to their room to listen to loud music, but run up against irritable parents who need peace and quiet. All of these needs and responses are understandable, but when they bump up against someone else's needs, they can lead to fractured relationships.

None of us likes to be out of relationship with those we love. Our young children are devastated when we are angry with them. Our older children may insist that they don't care, but the truth is they are miserable until the relationship is restored. We adults are similarly affected. We are not able to concentrate on our work or enjoy leisure if those we care about are hostile toward us.

   1. What situations in your family tend to cause broken relationships? List the "top ten."
   2. What consequences of broken relationships do you see in other families? Separation and divorce? Abuse? Illness? What are the consequences in your own family?

1. We Can Treat Others as Persons.

What specific suggestions did Jesus and the early church writers give us about how to avoid breaking relationships and how to heal those that are broken? Many of Jesus' teachings are concerned with this question and are summed up in Luke 6:27- 31, ending with the Golden Rule: "As you wish that [others] would do to you, do so to them." In other words, Jesus was saying that we should treat others as persons with the same kinds of feelings that we have, and not as things.

If we view people as things to be manipulated, like pieces in a chess game, we begin to believe that we can't hurt them, for they don't have feelings. All of us know of the historic results of this kind of thinking— slavery, the treatment of women as property, persecution of the Jews. Yet I have seen parents who are against all these horrors treat their children in the same way. They have criticized them in front of others as though they were deaf or not present. They have assaulted them with damaging words that they wouldn't think of saying to someone they care less about than they do their children, not realizing what the child may be feeling.

Spouses sometimes receive the same kind of treatment. We lash out in anger with words to our mates that we wouldn't think of using with a friend or stranger. Jesus had some strong things to say about the use of insulting words when we become angry. Matthew records his saying, "Whoever insults his brother shall be liable to the council, and whoever says, 'You fool!' shall be liable to the hell of fire" (Matt. 5:22). Paul also wrote, "Do not use harmful words in talking. Use only helpful words, the kind that build up and provide what is needed, so that what you say will do good to those who hear you" (Eph. 4:29, TEV). If we would follow this advice, how many broken relationships could be avoided!

Respond to feelings.

If we see others as feeling persons, not things, we can respond to their feelings instead of just their words or actions. Sometimes trying to sense what another is feeling takes creative imagination. If we are dealing with a child or youth, it helps to remember what it was like for us at that age.

In a young mother's discussion group one of the women expressed concern over her three-year-old daughter who was having temper tantrums. The mother was expecting a third child shortly and was preparing the three-year-old for the new arrival by telling her what a big girl she was and how much help she would be with the new baby.

The leader asked, "If you were only three, had been a baby only a short time when a baby brother came along and took over your mother's attention, and now there was going to be another baby to rob you further of attention, and in addition you were expected to help with it, how would you feel?" The mother was able to become that three-year-old for a moment and feel what she felt. She answered quietly, "Overwhelmed, scared, resentful." Then she understood the child's behavior and how to deal with it.

As adults we sometimes ignore or deny what children are feeling in an attempt to correct behavior or talk them out of a bad mood. To the four-year-old who doesn't like having his truck taken away from him we say, "You don't need to cry. You've been playing with that truck for an hour. It's time to share." To the eight-year-old who comes home from school angry at the teacher for taking away recess, we sermonize, "Don't blame the teacher. It was your fault." To the teenager who uses abusive language about the friend who has been mean, we admonish with our worn-out maxim, "If you can't say something nice, don't say anything at all."

We are afraid that if we acknowledge what the person is feeling we will encourage the behavior. Certainly we want our children to be unselfish, to be respectful of teachers, to refrain from gossiping and using foul language. However, to acknowledge what they are feeling and help them put a name to it without judgment releases them from the power of the emotion.

"It's disappointing to give up a toy that you are having so much fun with." "It's humiliating to have to sit in the classroom and work while everyone else is out playing." "It hurts to have a friend turn against you." When we do this, we say to the child, "I understand what you are feeling." Then they are free to change the behavior themselves.

Unacknowledged feelings hang around crying to be recognized, and the behavior is more likely to continue until the feeling is responded to.

If we can learn to respond to feelings without criticism as soon as they occur, we can avoid this kind of domestic strife that sometimes ends in violence. "Do not let the sun go down on your anger" (Eph.

4:26) is wise counsel, pointing out the advisability of taking care of negative feelings right away.

    3. *You have probably witnessed parents treating their children as objects. Recall some examples, both blatant and subtle. How could you help such parents?*
    4. *Examine a recent situation where your child exhibited negative feelings. What do you think were the causes? How did you respond? How could you have responded?*

2. We Can Love Ourselves.

We also need to treat ourselves as persons, not things. The last half of the Great Commandment emphasizes this: "Love your neighbor as yourself" (Matt. 22:39). This love of self is not selfish or egotistical love but a recognition that we too, imperfect as we are, are children of God, valued and worthy of love.

If we are conscientious parents, we often fall prey to berating ourselves for our failures. We feel guilty for so many things—not giving our children enough time, being impatient, losing our tempers. If we don't feel good about ourselves, we may make it difficult for those we live with. For one thing we tend to demand that our children be perfect to make up for our shortcomings. What a load that places on them!

The same principles of treating others as feeling persons can be applied to our treatment of ourselves. We need to acknowledge our own feelings without judgments. For instance, most of us would not think of scolding a child who comes home with hurt feelings. We know that he or she is already feeling bad enough. Yet we do this to ourselves. "I know it's wrong to feel so angry." "I hate myself for feeling jealous."

Such inner lashings inflict more wounds and add to our stress. If we are already hurting too much, we will deny the feeling. "I'm not angry; I'm just hurt." Somehow we need to learn that feelings are not moral issues. They need no judgments, and we need have no fear of calling them by their real names.

So let us be gentle with ourselves. So often we are harder on ourselves than others are, and certainly harder than God is. God loves us with all of our failures and shortcomings and can enable us to love ourselves without conditions. When we can do this, healing can take place within us, and we can then love others as we love ourselves.

> 5. *When do you find it most difficult to love yourself? How does this contribute to broken relationships? At such times, what healing do you need?*

3. We Can Listen.

Another recommendation for keeping in good relationship that has its roots in the Christian faith is what psychologists call "active listening." Jesus, of course, didn't call it this, but he did speak about people having ears to hear and about how people hear but don't understand. He himself practiced active listening, often hearing "beneath" people's words what they were feeling and saying nonverbally. For instance, when Martha spoke sharply to him about her sister Mary's not helping, he heard beneath her critical words, "I'm anxious about getting everything done." He responded to that rather than to her sharp words (Luke 10:40-41).

In the letter of James we read some advice about listening: "Let every [person] be quick to hear, slow to speak, slow to anger" (James 1:19). How many broken relationships could be avoided if we listened first and really heard what another was saying before we spoke!

I know of a situation in which a daughter hated school and caused her parents a great deal of stress by her constant "illnesses" that prevented her from going. If they made her go, there would often be a call from the school nurse saying she had a headache or stomach ache and would they come pick her up. One morning she was to take an important test. When she didn't get up on time, the mother went into her room, and the girl announced, "I'm not going."

Suddenly the mother "heard" what she was really saying. "I'm scared I won't be able to answer the questions." Instead of reprimanding the girl or trying to reason with her, she simply said quietly, "It's frightening not to be able to answer the questions, isn't it? It makes you feel dumb." The girl responded with tear-filled eyes and a nod of the head. Then together they sought some alternatives to solve the problem.

We do not become active listeners overnight, especially if we have spent a lifetime responding to people's words and actions on a literal level. It takes time to unlearn something and determination to try a different response. Our children and mates will no doubt give us many opportunities to practice.

Our response, of course, depends a great deal on how tired we are, how much stress we are under, how much time we have at the moment. However, no matter how rushed we are, there is always time to wait a few seconds before responding, trying to hear what is being said beneath angry words and actions. The biblical injunction in James is valid: "Be quick to hear, slow to speak, slow to anger."

> 6. What listening skills do you want to develop further? How could you practice these?

4. We Can Make the First Move.

Jesus had another recommendation for healing relationships that, if followed, would make a difference in dealing with family stress. Following his warning about the danger of using insulting words, he said, "So if you are offering your gift at the altar, and there remember that your brother has something against you, leave your gift there before the altar and go: first be reconciled to your brother, and then come and offer your gift" (Matt. 5:23-24). Jesus was saying that whenever there is a broken relationship, we are to make the first move toward reconciliation. Furthermore, we must do this before we can be in relationship with God. Our relationships with people and God are inseparable.

If we want to hear what people are really saying, sometimes we have to ask for their angry words. We have to find out what it is that is causing them to be upset with us. Such confrontation is scary and risky. The alternative, however, is living in an atmosphere of sullenness, oppressive silence, or back-biting remarks. This is not healthy for anyone.

Those who have difficulty in expressing their emotional hurts out loud need to be enabled to do this. One way is to verbalize what we think the person is feeling. "I sense you are angry with me. "I hurt your feelings last night, didn't I?" If we are wrong, hopefully they will tell us, and that too will open up the communication.

Sometimes we may have to take the initiative and express how we are feeling in order to help the other person share. If we do this, it is well to use "I" messages and not put the blame on the other person.

"I'm feeling unhappy because of our disagreement." "I'm upset because we can't talk to each other." An apology never hurts even if we feel the problem isn't all our fault. "I'm sorry about what I said yesterday." "I know I shouldn't have pushed you to go to the party."

It doesn't even hurt to admit to a child that we are wrong. Some parents may feel that this is a sign of weakness, that to apologize to a child will make them lose control of the situation, but this is not true. It is treating the child like a person with feelings and teaches by example how to help relationships heal. Whatever it takes to get a person to express what they are angry about, it is worth trying it to open up the lines of communication again. Jesus said it is up to us to make the first move toward reconciliation.

7. How difficult it often is to make the first move! Is there a situation you are now facing where your initiative could lead to healing?

5. We Can Forgive.

One of the reasons we hesitate to make the first move is that we are afraid of the confrontation. We may have to hear some things we don't want to hear. We may already know that we are partially to blame and be hurting inside from our own guilt. The truth is that all of us stand in need of forgiveness. The Christian knows how and where forgiveness can be found.

Jesus was very clear about this, and again he linked the forgiveness of people to the forgiveness of God. Following the Lord's prayer in Matthew, which includes forgiving others, he says: "For if you forgive [others] their trespasses, your heavenly Father also will forgive you; but if you do not forgive [others] their trespasses, neither will your Father forgive your trespasses (Matt. 6:14-15). His parable of the unforgiving servant (Matt. 18:23-35) says the same thing, and it does not have a happy ending. Furthermore, he doesn't give us any escape clauses. "And when you stand and pray, forgive *anything* you may have against *anyone*, so that your Father in heaven will forgive the wrongs you have done" (Mark 11:25).

Stress caused by carrying around guilt or bitterness can be damaging both emotionally and physically. Forgiving those who have wronged us takes away the bitterness. Being forgiven relieves us of the burden of guilt. The forgiveness of God is always available whenever we are truly sorry and ask to be taken back into relationship, but we cannot receive God's forgiveness if we are out of relationship with others or if we refuse to forgive ourselves, for we are all linked together. What profound wisdom Jesus had!

Helping children forgive

Children also need models of forgiving parents so they themselves can learn to forgive. There are many ills in their world today that call for forgiveness. Divorce is one. In a confirmation class one of the boys shared how resentful he was when his parents got a divorce. He was angry at them and at God. "I prayed for them to stay together," he said, "but they got divorced anyway." In a junior high Sunday school class I gave students a list of circumstances that can cause changes in a family and asked them to rate them from the easiest to the most difficult to adjust to. Almost all of them rated divorce as one of the most difficult. They gave it the same rating as death.

Psychologists point out that many children blame themselves when their parents get divorced. They need help in understanding that it is not their fault. Often children become bitter toward one parent against the other, and parents who are themselves resentful can foster this attitude. This is not helpful to the child. If the parents remarry, the children's adjustment to stepparents can be made difficult if the bitterness caused by the divorce has not been dealt with and forgiven.

Moving is another hardship on children, especially older children and teenagers. Whenever possible we should include them in the discussion and decision to move. If the move is in the summer, it helps to let them return to visit friends in the former place of residence or have the friends visit them. Spending extra time with them, being sensitive and supportive in their loneliness and sense of loss, encouraging them to get involved in friend-making activities and groups are all ways to make the adjustment easier and lessen the resentment.

How to forgive

Few serious Christians would argue with the necessity of forgiving others, but it is not easy to do. First we have to admit to our anger and take care of it. It does no good to give mere lip service to "I forgive you." If we can tell the person who has hurt us that we are angry and why, this often takes care of the resentment before it builds. Of course we need to express our anger without insult; otherwise both parties may end up with more things to forgive.

We can express our anger even to a young child with a simple statement such as, "I'm angry at you, Jonathan, for disobeying me. I want to be left alone now for a few minutes." Again this kind of response not only keeps us from using damaging words but serves as a model to help children deal with their own angers and resentments. Another technique to help us forgive is an exercise based on 1 Corinthians 13:5b: "Love does not keep a record of wrongs" (TEV). When we have been hurt many times by someone, we may begin to keep a mental list. Finally the last offense on the list, even a small one, becomes the last straw.

If we are dealing with resentment that has built up over a period of time, it might help to write down the list of wrongs. Then tear it up. Writing the list down is a way to get in touch with the anger. Tearing it up is a symbolic way of getting rid of it. We can also encourage our children who are old enough to write to use this technique.

Finally, we can take our anger to God in prayer, but again it does no good to be dishonest with ourselves or God. I usually pray something like this: "God, I'm so angry at _____ that I can't stand him right now. I know you love him and care about him. Help me to see him the way you do." I may have to pray like this for several days or weeks, depending on the nature of the offense, but eventually the anger subsides, God's love pours in, and I am able to forgive.

> 8. *What kinds of behavior do you find hardest to forgive? What persons? Would expressing your anger help? Tearing up a list of wrongs? Prayer? What new steps will you take in forgiving others?*
>
> 9. *Consider your answers to Question 1 again. Based on your insights from this chapter, how can you become a healing influence in each of these situations?*

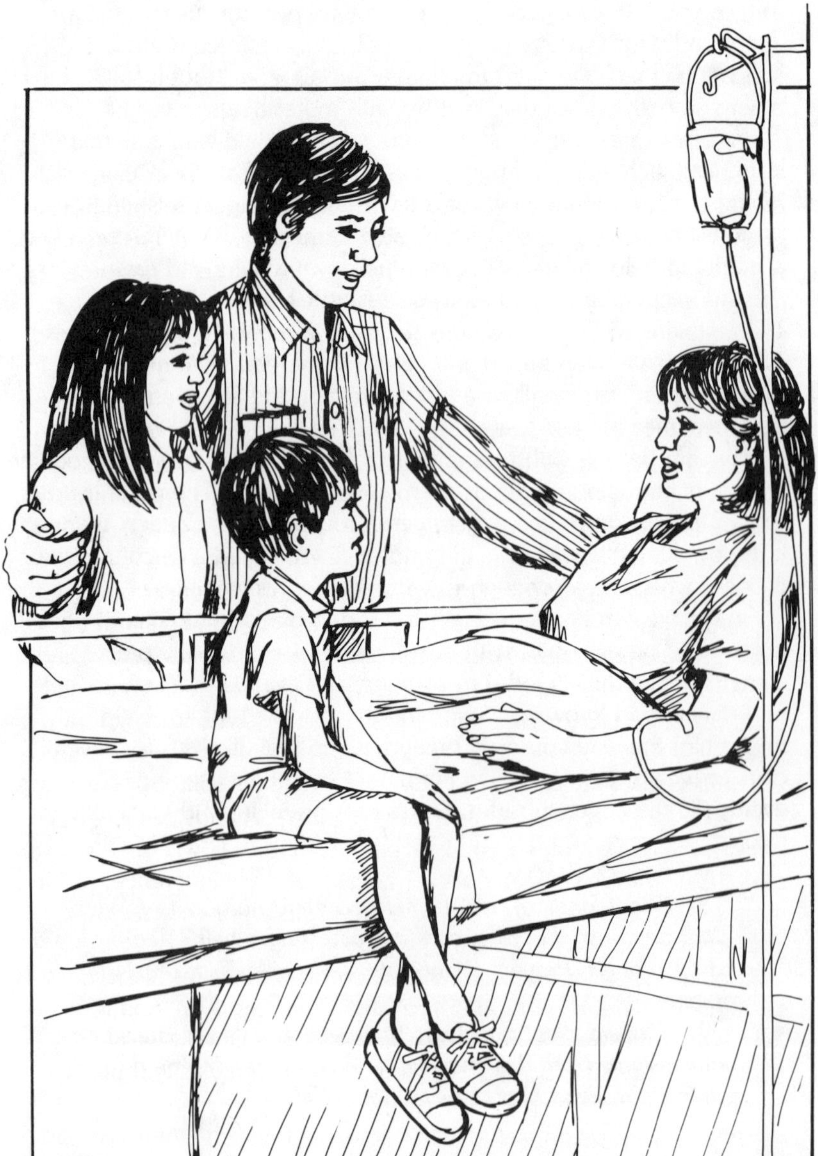

Chapter Six

COPING WITH ILLNESS AND DEATH

There is yet another stress that some have to deal with in their parenting—the serious illness and/or death of a spouse or child. This is perhaps the most devastating of all crises and the most difficult to cope with. No one really understands the pain of this kind of experience without going through it themselves. It is one thing to accept the inevitability of the death of an aged parent, but quite another to face the disability or death of a young person or child.

How can the Christian faith help parents and children move through these kinds of crises with faith and courage? Is it possible to believe in a God of love when such things happen? Can we still affirm that "in all things God works for good" when, for example, leukemia claims the life of a child or a drunken driver kills a young father?

The kind of help we receive through faith in the face of such tragedies depends to a great extent again on our concept of God. If we see God as the cause of suffering, we will not find religion to be helpful. A woman who had just received word that a close friend had a child who was dying of an incurable illness said to me in anger and bitterness, "Who does God think he is, to do this kind of thing to a child?"

The late Leslie Weatherhead spoke to this in his spiritual classic, *The Will of God*. Speaking to a friend whose son had died in a cholera epidemic and who had called his death the "will of God," he said, "Call your little boy's death the result of mass ignorance, call it mass folly, call it mass sin, . . . call it bad drains or communal carelessness, but don't call it the will of God."[5]

Another stumbling block to faith when disaster strikes is the seeming indifference of God. Once on a plane trip I sat next to a man who in the course of our conversation discovered I was a minister's wife. After a period of silence he suddenly asked me, "Does God have a heart?"

Behind his question was a recent tragedy in which a little girl had been raped, then brutally beaten. He was asking some age-old questions: Where was God? Why didn't God stop this from happening? He went on to comment, "I have a heart, and if I had been there I would have done everything I could to keep this from happening."

1. *You probably know some families who have lived through devastating crises—serious injury, illness, death. Recall their attitudes toward God at the time. Did any blame God for causing the problem, or for not caring? What other attitudes were evident?*

1. We Can Depend on God.

Seeing God as the cause of disasters or as indifferent to suffering is an understandable response, for which there is no easy answer, particularly if the disaster is happening to us. This is why it is better to give serious thought to our concepts of God in times of calm rationality rather than when disaster strikes and emotions take over.

I believe that the reason God does not intervene is related to the nature of the universe and the way God has created it. It is a dependable universe based on physical laws. It is my conviction that a God who breaks natural laws for individual requests could not be depended upon; the universe itself would soon be out of control under such a system. What a chaotic world we would have if, for instance, we never knew if the law of gravity would operate if we jumped from a ten-story building! Because we know what will happen, the choice to cooperate with gravity or defy it is ours.

When natural disasters such as earthquakes or tornadoes occur, if we happen to be in their path we will suffer. If germs are around (part of God's evolving creation too) and our resistance is down, we will become ill. If we drink too much alcohol certain physical laws operate in our bodies, and we become drunk. The consequences of this behavior will affect others if they are in our path.

Of course, if we believe that there is an intelligent designer behind the universe, whom religious people call God, we can still call all these tragedies the will of God. However, I believe God also created us with free will, and in many cases it is our choices or someone else's that cause the suffering, as in the case of the child who was raped. God does not interfere with our free will or else we would be robots. However, God can use this freedom of choice (if *we* choose) to bring us through suffering and sorrow to wholeness.

Weatherhead points out that God's intentional will, which is always good, may be thwarted by circumstances—people's misguided or evil actions, disease, natural disasters, etc.—but God's ultimate will is never defeated. "When we say, then, that God is omnipotent, we do not mean that nothing can happen unless it is God's will. We mean that nothing can happen which can *finally* defeat [God]."[6]

    2. Consider a recent crisis faced by your family or someone you know. What would you say was "God's will" for the situation? God's will for the persons involved? In what sense could the people rely on a dependable God?

2. God Suffers with Us.

How then does faith help to see us through to healing when our lives are shattered by tragedies? The answer lies in another aspect to our Christian belief in a personal God—the idea of God as sufferer, the belief that God suffers with us in those devastating experiences of life over which we have no control.

Jesus demonstrated this in his ministry as he strove by example to show what God is like. He wept with people in their sorrows. In the account of Lazarus' death, John records, "When Jesus saw [Martha] weeping, and the Jews who came with her also weeping, he was deeply moved in spirit and troubled. . . . Jesus wept" (John 11:33, 35).

Furthermore, Jesus demonstrated his faith in a suffering God by his acceptance of an unexpected kind of messiahship. Most of the Jews of his day were expecting a military Messiah; instead Jesus felt his mission to be the suffering servant of Isaiah: "Surely he has borne our griefs and carried our sorrows" (Isa. 53:4).

All of us know what it means to have someone care enough to cry with us. It doesn't take away the pain, but it helps lift the load, making it bearable. It takes away the isolation. I was alone once in a hospital dining room, seeking physical nourishment during a vigil with a dying loved one. All around me were people laughing and visiting. No one knew me or my sorrow. No one cared. I fled in tears, seeking the hospital chaplain. I needed someone who could put me in touch with a God who cares.

The Christian faith, when it is understood at its depth, also offers comfort from someone who knows about suffering. At the heart of its message is a crucifixion, the ultimate in cruelty, suffering, and loss. In the Christian drama there is no Greek god in a machine who comes down and interferes with people's evil choices or with natural laws. This is why the story of Jesus has always spoken to the suffering, why the slave could sing with such conviction:

> Nobody knows the trouble I've seen,
> Nobody knows but Jesus.

However, in the Christian drama the crucifixion is not the final word. At the heart of our faith is also the resurrection. Whatever we may believe or disbelieve about the resurrection, the fact is that it was a reality for the disciples and early Christians and gave them courage to spread the faith and face death because of it. In their experience they and God were not defeated by death.

> 3. *Do you believe that when you suffer, God suffers with you? Do you sense the presence of this suffering God?*
> 4. *At the time of death, how does the story of Jesus' suffering, death, and resurrection speak to you? What could you do to get in touch with this story at a deeper level?*

3. God Is Our Friend.

How does faith in a God who cares about us and suffers with us in our distress help when, for instance, we receive the news that a child has a disabling or incurable disease or that a spouse has been critically injured in an accident? Our faith tells us that this God is our friend, not our enemy, that we can depend upon God to give us wisdom and serenity and an enabling power to accept what cannot be changed.

These are the tools we need when a crisis of this magnitude crashes into our lives. Sometimes the inner wisdom we are given leads us to a particular doctor or clinic, to someone who has had a similar experience, to some knowledge about treatment or medication. An inner calmness enables us to become a channel for healing for our loved one. Tenseness in us and in the injured is a block to healing. This is why doctors prescribe pain medicine and tranquilizers; the body heals quickest when it is relaxed. We facilitate this for someone else when we ourselves are at peace.

Acceptance of what cannot be changed is perhaps the hardest task of all. It comes slowly, and only after we have dealt with denial, anger, bargaining with God, and depression—that is, the stages of the grief process (as outlined by Elizabeth Kübler-Ross). Many people get stuck in one of these stages, but a belief in a God who cares can enable us to move through each of them to healing, either emotional or physical or both.

I do not know how this happens, but I do know that through the power of the Holy Spirit in some mysterious way it does. The testimonies to this are myriad. Two specific instances come to mind. A bright high school girl among our acquaintances was critically injured when her car was hit by a logging truck, leaving her permanently brain-damaged and confined to a wheelchair. During this heartbreaking experience her parents, who were persons of faith, came to accept what could not be changed, expressed gratitude for the healing that did take place, and adapted their mode of living to this changed circumstance in their lives.

In another instance a neighbor of ours had to deal with the shattering discovery that her husband had lung cancer. At first she was devastated; then she came to accept it and through God's power was given the ability to minister to him to the end. She told me she was amazed at how she was able to do this with a sense of joy in her heart, even while she was deeply saddened.

Does this mean we should not pray for a loved one to be healed but only for acceptance? No. Our prayers for healing are necessary. However, demands for physical healing may thwart God's ability to help us through these kinds of experiences, because we do not always know the kind of healing that is needed or possible. A trust in a God who cares deeply about us and our loved ones can turn our frantic demands or desperate pleas into a calm assurance that good will emerge. We can trust that within the dependable framework of God's physical and spiritual laws, some kind of healing will take place. As always, we are given a choice. We can fight God and the circumstance, or we can trust God to work for good within it.

> 5. *For those who depend on God in times of severe crisis, what gifts does God have? In what ways does the Spirit enable hope and healing? Examine a recent experience of yours, or of a friend's, for clues.*

4. We Can Help Children Deal with Illness and Death.

When tragedy strikes a family member, children are deeply affected by it. If it is hard for us adults to understand why bad things happen to good people, it is even more difficult for a child. The most logical one to blame is God. Russell Baker in his autobiography, *Growing Up*, recounts his own experience at five when his father died.

Speaking of his family he wrote, "With a thousand tasks to do, they had no time to handle a howling five-year-old. I was sent to the opposite end of town, to Bessie Scott's house. For the first time I thought seriously about God. Between sobs I told Bessie that if God could do things like this to people, then God was hateful and I had no more use for Him.

"Bessie said I would understand someday, but she was only partly right. That afternoon . . . I decided that God was a lot less interested in people than anybody in Morrisonville was willing to admit. That day I decided that God was not entirely to be trusted. After that I never cried again with any real conviction, nor expected much of anyone's God except indifference."[7]

As parents how can we help our children and young people deal with illness and death in such a way that their faith is strengthened rather than shattered? For one thing, we need to include them in the experience rather than sending them away or becoming silent when they come around. Children know when something has happened. They are often frightened and bewildered. To add isolation to this only compounds their stress instead of alleviating it. Being sad together brings comfort and is a bonding experience.

It is also important to be honest with children. How much and how we tell a child about his or her own serious illness or the condition of a family member depends, of course, on the age of the child. If a child has questions, however, we need to answer them as honestly as we can without causing fear. If unusual treatment or surgery is required, we can make it less traumatic by talking about what to expect. Always the child needs to know that we will be there. Also we need to encourage the youngster to express his or her feelings, especially fears and sorrow, so the child will not have to deal with them in total isolation.

One of the saddest experiences my husband has had in his ministry was with a fourteen-year-old boy who had leukemia. The parents were afraid to tell him, nor would they let anyone else. He was an intelligent youth who knew he was dying, yet he couldn't talk about it to anyone. He ended his life a very lonely boy. His church friends all said afterwards that if they had a terminal illness they would want to know so they could talk about it and prepare themselves for what lay ahead.

Prayers of trust

Another way we can help children cope with illness and death is to teach them how to pray. Their natural inclination, and ours, is to make demands on God. If their prayers are not answered as requested, their faith is shattered. "It didn't do any good to pray. My brother died anyway." If, however, we pray prayers of trust with them, we will calm their spirits and ours and make it possible for God to work for good in the situation.

If we pray prayers of trust with children all through their growing years, we will bring them into an abiding relationship with God and away from any tendency to use God for their own ends. This will stand them in good stead all their lives. We can do this kind of praying when childhood tragedies, which seem like major disasters to them, come into their experience.

For example, when one of our boys was small, his pet hampster was mauled by the cat. He wanted to pray that God not let his pet die. I, who could see that the hampster was mortally wounded, was concerned that this unanswered demand might affect his faith. I suggested rather that we trust God to do what was best, which might be death rather than suffering. When the hampster died during the night, our son was not unduly distressed.

Sharing our faith

There are many fine books written on coping with death—the death of a child or a spouse, explaining death to a child, etc. (see Resources, p. 75). However, the best way a parent can help a child through the pain of losing a loved one is by living and sharing his or her own faith in a personal God who cares for us in every experience of life, including death.

In his book, *Disciplines of the Spirit*, Howard Thurman gives testimony to this. He tells about an experience in his childhood when he was awakened by his mother to go outside to see Halley's comet. "There I saw in the heavens the awesome tail of the comet and stood transfixed. With deep anxiety I asked, . . . What will happen to us when that thing falls out of the sky?'

"There was a long silence during which I felt the gentle pressure of her fingers on my shoulders; then I looked into her face and saw what I had seen on another occasion, when without knocking I had rushed into her room and found her in prayer. At last she said, 'Nothing will happen to us, Howard. God will take care of us.' In that moment something was touched and kindled in me, a quiet reassurance that has never quite deserted me. As I look back on it, what I sensed then was the fact that what stirred in me was one with what created and controlled the comet."[8]

To be at one with God is to be whole, no matter how shattered our world is. This is not to deny or minimize the pain of sorrow and loss. It is to face it realistically with the One who created us out of love and whom we can trust to see us through.

This was affirmed centuries ago by the Apostle Paul, who knew from his own experience: "Who shall separate us from the love of Christ? Shall tribulation, or distress, or persecution, or famine, or nakedness, or peril, or sword? No, in all these things we are more than conquerors through him who loved us. For I am sure that neither death, nor life, . . . nor things present, nor things to come, . . . nor anything in all creation will be able to separate us from the love of God in Christ Jesus our Lord" (Rom. 8:35, 37-39).

> 6. *Based on this section and your own experience, list eight or ten principles to guide you in helping children deal with the serious illness or death of others. What would you change or add for children who face illness or death themselves?*
>
> 7. *You might prepare for prayer with your children by writing out what you would like to pray with them in possible crisis situations—the death of a pet, serious hospitalization of a friend, death of a relative.*
>
> 8. *Perhaps it is at times of crisis that our faith is most evident to our children. How did you share your faith at some recent crisis? How would you like to be able to do so next time?*

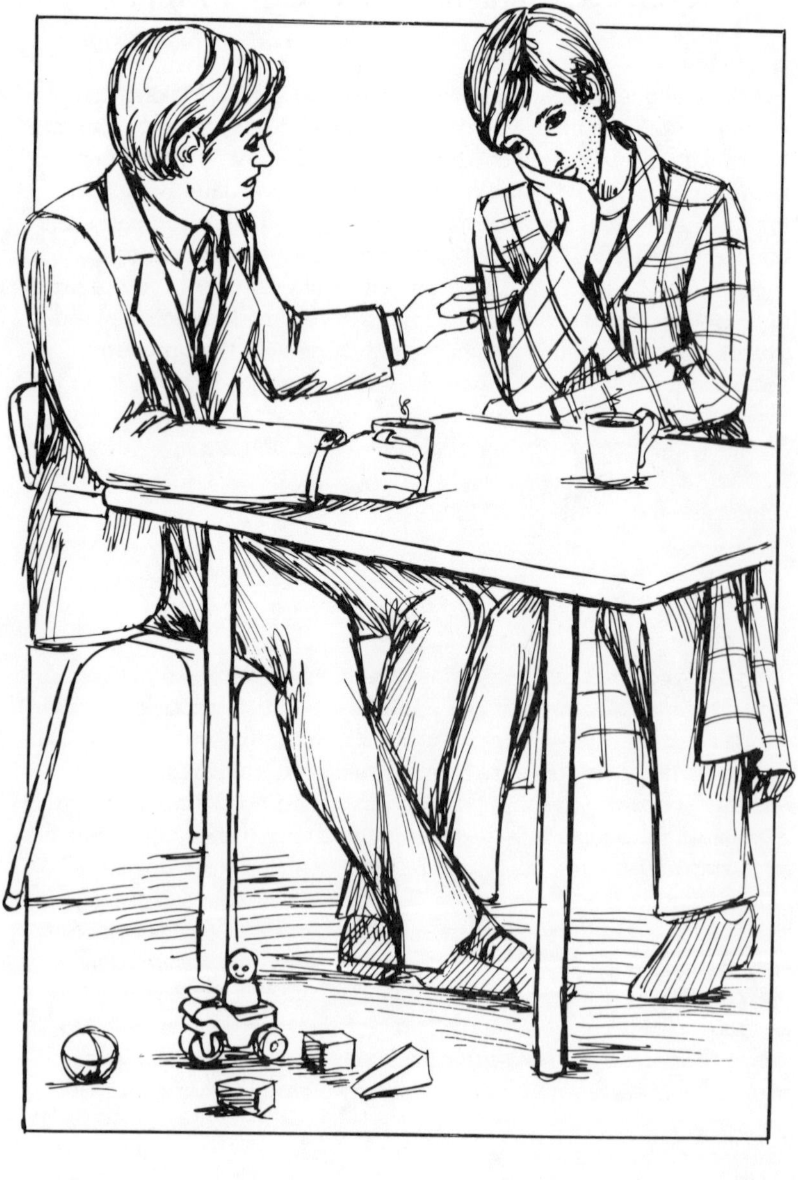

Chapter Seven

WITH A LITTLE HELP FROM OUR COMMUNITY OF FAITH

The setting is Sunday morning, Anywhere, U.S.A. Making their way to church are three new families. There is Ken, a newly divorced father, with his two small children. There is Darlene, pushing her paralyzed son in a wheelchair. There are Neil and Jane Kelly and their two teenagers, recently transferred by Mr. Kelly's company and ethnically different from most of the people in the community.

All of these people are living with stressful experiences. What kind of welcome will they find at the church? Will they find warmth and acceptance and resources to help them cope with their present circumstances? What will those of us who are actively involved in the faith community do to meet the needs of these and all others who are seeking a caring relationship with fellow Christians? In short, what kind of help can the community of faith offer parents who are dealing with stress and crisis?

1. A Community of Shared Belief

The faith community makes significant contributions in helping us face the stress of today's world. For one thing, it offers support when we take a moral stand. For example, a group of young mothers sponsored by a church were sharing their concerns about today's society. One woman said, "Frankly, I'm scared about my marriage. Almost all the people who work in my husband's office are separated or divorced. They are all sleeping around and think nothing of it."

Her fears were well-founded. Not long after this her husband decided he wanted his freedom and was planning to move out. She was distraught. They saw a marriage counselor who recommended that she attend a support group for women who were separated or divorced. She did so and came back to the church group with this report: "They were all bitter against men. The books they recommended and discussed advocated sleeping around, swapping partners, paying your husband back for what he had done to you. It all seemed so wrong to me."

It is very difficult to hold on to our values if we are surrounded by people who hold a different view. If everyone at the office is doing it, if everyone in the neighborhood says there's nothing wrong with it, pretty soon we begin to wonder if there's something wrong with us. This is not to say the church should have a holier-than-thou attitude and sit in judgment on those whose lifestyles are different. It does mean that if something seems right or wrong for us, we need the support of like-minded people to help us keep our stand.

Moral values include many areas besides our personal behavior. Equally important are our values related to such social issues as racism, sexism, world peace, concern for the environment, to mention a few. As parents we try to teach Christian values to our children, and they run up against the same kind of opposition from others as we do.

Sometimes the stands they take lead to persecution. For instance, a child who is friends with someone of a different race may be shunned by fellow classmates. A youth who refuses to cheat or take drugs may be teased or ostracized by peers. Our children and youth need the support of their church friends if they take a Christian stand on a social or moral issue.

Strength for faith convictions

This is true not only of our moral convictions but also for our faith convictions. There are those who maintain that a person can be a good Christian without the fellowship of the church. "Faith is a personal response between an individual and God," they say. This is absolutely true, but it is extremely difficult to keep the flame of faith alive without the support of like-minded individuals. This is why God not only calls us individually, but also into a community of others who are also responding to God's call.

You may have heard the story of the Scottish pastor who called on one of his parishioners who had been absent from worship for several Sundays. The pastor found his backsliding member sitting beside his fireplace in which the coals were burning brightly. When he spoke to him about missing services, the parishioner said, "Aye, Pastor, but I can worship God just as well here by my fire as I can in church." At this the pastor pulled a burning coal out from the pile of coals, and together they sat there in silence as the single coal, separated from the heat of its fellows, began to die out. The flame of faith in each of us needs to be fed by the body of believers.

1. How has your congregation empowered and supported you in relation to personal moral issues? Social issues? What could your faith community do to be more helpful?

2. How has it supported you in your Christian convictions? What further support do you need?

2. A Community of Fellowship and Growth

Another contribution the community of faith gives us is a social fellowship. It is a place to make friends. We live in a highly mobile society, and one of the main causes of stress is moving. Pulling up roots, leaving behind family and friends is a little like death, and the first few months in a new community can be very lonely and depressing. It can be especially difficult if we are adults who are not employed outside the home and don't have the opportunity to meet people at work.

The faith community, if we are doing our job, reaches out with a warm welcome to newcomers. It provides fellowship groups— youth groups, groups for post-high young people, young couples, singles, single parents. If there are persons in our congregation with special needs, such as the mentally retarded or physically handicapped, we may be moved to help them form a group. Sometimes there are not enough people in one of these categories in one church to make up a fellowship group, so several churches may go together to form a needed group. This can be especially helpful for single young adults who are lonely for fellowship but who don't want to seek friendships in places like bars or "swinging" singles' groups.

Growth groups

Along with fellowship we in the church can also provide opportunities for intellectual and spiritual growth. Such traditional settings as church school classes and Bible study and prayer groups nurture our religious development. In addition, the issues of our time need to be addressed in the light of the faith. Here the possibilities are endless.

One church I know offered a series of Saturday afternoon seminars every two weeks through the summer, using those with expertise both within and outside its membership as leaders. They covered a range of topics: Living with the Sexual Revolution, Stress Management, Death and Dying, A Look at Racism, Religious Cults.

We can offer a six-week course during Lent or at other times of the year in a particular area of concern such as alcoholism, drug abuse, world hunger, influence of television, world peace. Often this kind of study leads to action and benefits the entire community. Study groups for parents of young children or of teenagers, for stepparents, for single parents, using current books as resources, can provide insights and support.

All of these are ways that the community of faith can help parents deal with the problems of modern living. If we see any of these needs in our church fellowship or community, perhaps God is calling us to do something about meeting them.

>   3.   How do you evaluate your congregation's work in providing for Christian fellowship and growth opportunities? Who is included and who left out? What changes would you make?

3. A Community of Support and Prayer

One of the most helpful services the church provides is support for families going through crisis situations. This takes many forms. A family struck by unemployment or a disaster such as fire or flood may need food, clothing, shelter to tide them over. When accident, serious illness, or death strikes, we in the faith community can bring in meals, clean the house, take care of children, and in other ways make things easier for those who bear the brunt of the strain.

Transportation to hospitals and doctors for medical treatment is another valuable service. For instance, a husband may be unable to get off work to take his wife for chemotherapy or radiation treatments. She may be able to drive, but this kind of treatment can be a lonely, frightening experience, in addition to causing physical illness or weakness. What a blessing to have church friends drive and relieve the loneliness and fear with spiritual and emotional support!

The ministry of prayer

Spiritual support during crises is the most significant contribution that the faith community can give. It is its unique offering. The secular world can and does offer physical and emotional assistance for many kinds of family crises. The church puts people in touch with God, the source of healing.

It does this in several ways. It offers the ministry of prayer. Many churches have a prayer chain that alerts people whenever there is a need. The beauty of prayer is that distance is no barrier. I can testify to this. Several years ago my husband and I were in a car accident several hundred miles from home. We were taken to the hospital in the nearest town, but I was critically injured and had to be transported to a larger city for emergency surgery. My husband immediately contacted the prayer chain in our local church. By the time I reached the hospital fifty miles away, prayers for healing were already coming my way. All through that experience I was so surrounded by love that I could sense it even though I was apart from friends and family. I was unafraid, relaxed, freed of stress, and I healed quickly.

When disaster strikes, panic usually grabs us by the throat. We may try to pray, but nothing comes except desperate pleas and a sense of hopelessness. At a time when we most urgently need to sense the presence of God, fear stands in the way and blocks God's calming Spirit. Then it is that the prayers of others do for us what we cannot do for ourselves. Those less emotionally involved undergird us and our loved ones with their prayerful concern. Our spirits are calmed, and we are able to be open to healing or to whatever is needful to see us through the crisis.

Weekly prayer groups provide support not only for people who are experiencing an acute crisis, but for those who are living under an ongoing stressful situation. In all the churches we have served, people have testified to the value of such groups. "When I was going through my divorce, I don't know what I would have done without the support of our prayer group." "When our little boy was dying of leukemia, knowing that people were praying for us every week got us through."

Most churches mention the names of those who are sick or have experienced the death of a loved one during the prayer time in the Sunday morning worship service. In addition, some churches hold healing services after the worship service or at some time during the week. Here those who are especially committed to this kind of ministry meet together to pray for those in need of healing in body, mind, or spirit. People are put in touch with God—and God, who knows where the healing needs to take place, is enabled by the support of others and the willingness of the suppliants to work for healing in people's lives.

The personal witness

In addition to prayer there are other kinds of spiritual support that the faith community can offer. Bruce Birch wrote of the support of the church when his little girl died: "The community helps to relieve the isolation suffered along with the anger and pain. A terrible sense of aloneness comes in the midst of such hardships; the community should surround us in those moments with a presence that is a witness to the presence of God."[9]

The secular world cannot do this. Only those who have experienced the presence of God can witness to it with authenticity. One way that some churches have done this is through a "crisis bank." When people join the church, the pastor asks if any of them have dealt with a crisis which they would be willing to share with others going through a similar experience. This could be a physical crisis—cancer, heart attack, organ transplant, loss of a limb. It could be an emotional crisis—divorce, loss of a child or a mate, mental illness, sexual abuse. It could be a crisis related to parenting—dealing with a terminal illness with a child, teenage pregnancy, abortion, drug abuse, homophobia.

The person willing to share fills out a confidential card with his or her name, address, phone number, and type of crisis. Only the pastor has access to it and uses it at his or her discretion when someone in the congregation has a similar problem. All of us know that the persons most helpful to call on in a crisis are those who have "been there" and have come through triumphantly.

The faith community as family

Finally, the community of faith offers us the same kind of support that a close-knit family does. Paul wrote to the Corinthians, "If one member suffers, all suffer together; if one member is honored, all rejoice together" (1 Cor. 12:26). Today much of our chronic stress is caused by separation and loneliness. Families are split apart by distance, by divorce, by differences in lifestyles, by a multitude of adjustments that our fast-changing society has made necessary. The church can ease this pain by providing a nurturing, caring community for people of all ages and stations.

In its intergenerational settings the congregation puts grandparents separated from their families in touch with substitute children and grandchildren. Young adults and their children who are missing their parents and grandparents benefit as they relate to older people and seek their wisdom and companionship. Holiday times can be made warm and joyous as members celebrate together at the church or are invited into each other's homes as surrogate grandparents, daughters, sons. Intergenerational family camps, picnics, and family nights provide fellowship and intellectual stimulation for all ages.

Older people in the church can provide babysitting services for young parents who are struggling financially, as they would do for their own children if they were living nearby. A group of dedicated women have done this twice a month for the young mother's groups I have led. A Parent's Day Out program is another service that many churches provide. Mothers and/or fathers can leave their children at the church for a nominal fee while they shop or simply have two or three hours to themselves to relieve the daily stress of parenting.

On the other hand, young people can provide services for senior citizens who may need help with housework, yard work, or transportation. A new generation of children is growing up deprived of the privilege of caring for the elderly, appreciating and understanding what it means to grow old and eventually die, as we all will. Families who "adopt" an older person, having them in their homes, taking them to church and community events as they would a grandparent, are doing themselves and their children a service.

  4. *In times of crisis, what kinds of support have you received from your church? And what have you offered others?*
  5. *Does your congregation provide transportation for those who need it? Regular prayer for those distressed? A crisis bank? Intergenerational fellowship? What new services could you help plan?*

4. We Care for Our Children and Youth.

The faith community also has a special ministry for its children and youth. It gives them an environment in which they cannot fail. So many times I have seen children and youth who are too shy or embarrassed to participate in music or drama at school shine in these areas at church. I have heard young people comment about the "wave of love" that comes up from the audience to support them when they are doing a play. Everyone there is pulling for them, wanting them to succeed. "They're *our* kids," the adults affirm. The world gives the young stressful competition, criticism, sometimes rejection. The church says, "You're all right! You belong!"

Churches that provide opportunities for children and youth to participate in its services and programs say to them, "You are as important as any adult. This is your church family. We need you." The ways children and youth can participate are numerous— choirs, acolytes, ushers, a children's time in the worship service, sharing from church school classes, serving on committees, helping with church dinners, service projects.

In the ritual for infant baptism both the parents and the congregation make certain vows. The parents promise to bring the child to church and to teach the faith by the example of their lives. The congregation promises to surround the child with steadfast love. If both parents and congregation live up to these vows, the children will become a part of the church family. Whatever happens to them, good or bad, becomes the concern of the entire congregation. They will contribute to their nurturing and help root them in the faith.

The sooner children are brought into the arena of the church fellowship and made to feel a part of it, the better are their chances to benefit from its nurture and influence. Children who grow up together from the nursery are more likely to keep these church friendships through the teen years when peer pressure is so strong. Church kids are not perfect, but statistics show that they are more likely to have strong moral values and a sense of purpose in their lives than those outside the church. This is good insurance against the kinds of stresses the adolescent years may bring.

These are all ways the faith community can help parents and children deal with the stresses of today's world, supporting and nurturing each family member through every age and life circumstance. This is the Body of Christ—his hands, his feet, his compassionate heart—caring for the world. Those of us who are touched by this caring fellowship will find within it the resources to help us cope with our own situations. Then by the Spirit's power we will be able to be the Body of Christ for others who come seeking help. This is the meaning and purpose of the beloved community.

5. List the ways your congregation cares for and supports its children and youth. Make another list of ways it cares for children and youth of the neighborhood and community. How do you evaluate these ministries? What's working well? What needs strengthening? What is missing altogether?

6. What one thing would you most like to do to help your congregation become more supportive of persons in situations of stress and crisis?

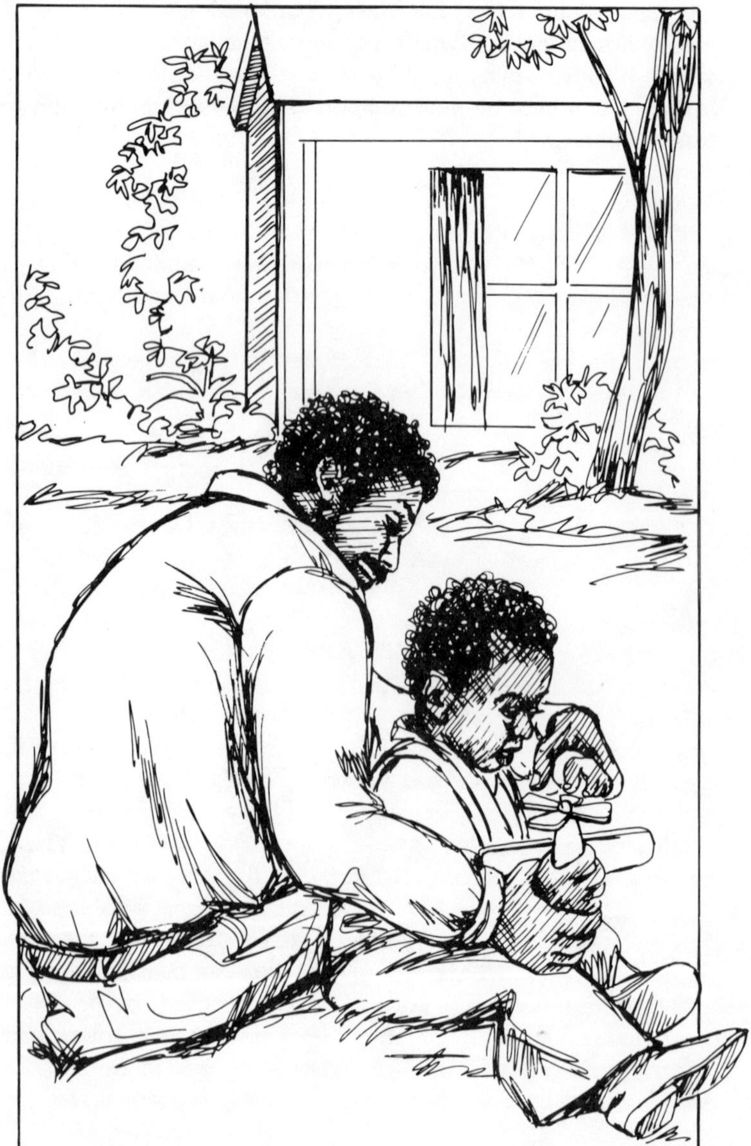

Chapter Eight

THE GOOD NEWS ABOUT THE BAD NEWS

Greg had just settled down to watch television when he was interrupted by the cries of his three-year-old son, Randy. "Now what?" he groaned to himself.

"Daddy, my airplane won't work," Randy sobbed as he handed Greg his cereal box plastic plane. "It's broke."

"Let me see," Greg said. He took the toy and examined it. "It's not broken, Randy. You just didn't have the rubber band tight enough to propel it. Here, let me show you."

"So much for my T.V. show," he thought ruefully to himself as he took his son into the backyard to give him an elementary lesson in physics.

1. Tension Creates Energy.

What Greg and Randy were doing, of course, was using tension to make the toy plane fly. In the physical world we do this all the time. Most mechanical things won't work without tension, from complex machinery to something as simple as a window shade which won't roll up if the spring isn't wound tightly inside the roller.

The same principle is true in our lives. It is tension that gives us the energy to get things done. It is a motivating force. There is the college student who works better when deadline pressure forces him to write his term paper. Public speakers and performers tell us that some nervousness and anxiety before facing an audience give them the energy to put forth their best effort. A certain amount of tension gives us a zest for living. A visit to a convalescent home for the elderly can verify this. Many people there have lost their desire to live because they have nothing or no one to be concerned about.

Think about the amount of energy that is generated in coping with the stresses of parenting. This is why parents are tired at the end of the day. The parent who works outside the home may think the homemaker does nothing but sit around all day. To correct this misconception, switch roles once in a while. When our children were small and my husband stayed home to babysit, he came up with an ingenious idea to allay his frustrations. He would make out a list of things he wanted to get done that day, but at the top of the list he always wrote: "Take care of kids." That way he could always scratch something off even if he didn't get to anything else. Parents who stay at home might do this each day, at least mentally.

For those who have young children, the day is full of airplanes that won't fly, fights that need arbitrating, bumps and scratches that need kissing. For those with school-age children the list may include chauffering, being a room parent, den mother, scout leader, plus coping with physical and emotional crises as well.

For those who may feel that in "just" being a housewife or a mother they haven't done anything, keeping a journal is one way to see how much gets accomplished each day. The tensions involved in parenting generate the energy that propels us through the day. This is one way to use stress to work for us rather than letting it work against us.

> 1. Recall some situations when stress seemed to energize you for action. And some when stress sapped your energy. What seems to make the difference? How can you use family stress as a source of energy?

2. Tension Holds Things Together.

Another use of tension in the physical world is for holding things together. It is the tightening up of a screw that keeps the table leg on. It is the pressing down on the spring and locking it in place that keeps the ballpoint pen together and makes it usable for writing. There is a device on a sewing machine called the *tension* that regulates the tautness of the thread. When it is malfunctioning, the stitches do not hold.

In our lives when we "fall apart," we usually make tension the culprit. Yet without a certain amount we would be useless. Parenting requires organization, planning the day's schedule, adjusting to the unexpected. When our children come to us with a physical or emotional problem, we help them cope by tightening up their emotional resources. We are also called upon many times to tighten up our own in order to keep ourselves or others from falling apart.

If we were totally relaxed, we would be indifferent to everyone's needs. This happened a few years ago when doctors prescribed the drug Valium too indiscriminately. Many housewives took it to help them get through the stress of the day so that nothing would phase them. As a result they sat around relaxed and sometimes indifferent to that which needed their attention. Tension makes us aware, keeps us alert, and when used creatively helps to keep our lives and those in our care running smoothly.

    2. What does it mean to "tighten up our emotional resources"? How does stress help you to hold things together?

3. Tension and Potential.

One of the dictionary definitions of *tension,* when used in respect to electricity, is "potential." This physical terminology can be applied to the constructive use of stress in our lives. As parents we are often aware that our children are not living up to their potential. A teacher may tell us that our son or daughter is an under-achiever, that he or she could do so much better. Experts have long been saying that the average human being uses only a fraction of her or his brain power.

If this is true in the physical world, it is also true in the spiritual. Using stress constructively is one means of helping us achieve our potential. In his book, *Stress, Distress, and Growth,* Dr. Walt Schafer illustrates this principle with an analogy of the sunflower seed. "Each sunflower seed possesses the potential to become a unique, fully developed, and beautiful plant. It has an innate drive to grow, to make that potential a reality. In its growth the plant faces many difficulties—soil to push through, the need for water and minerals, gravity, wind, sunlight that times is too bright—at others too dim.

"If conditions are right, the sunflower seed unfolds to become a magnificent flowering plant. Its potential has been realized—*because* it overcame stressful conditions as it matured. It is important to note that in order to grow, the plant needed these stressful conditions—up to a point. Challenges, as long as they are not too great, stimulate rather than retard growth."[10]

There is always something to unfold in us. As Christians we believe that we are called to become what God intends us to be. In fact, we are each called to be like God. Jesus said, "You, therefore, must be perfect, as your heavenly Father is perfect" (Matt. 5:48). Our potential is infinite. The dreams we have for ourselves and our children are nothing compared to the dreams God has for our lives.

We will not begin to realize this potential if we do not accept the challenges that life gives us. These challenges are gifts, in fact tools to aid us in our task of becoming what we are meant to be. If we tranquilize ourselves whenever difficulties arise or refuse to deal with them, we are refusing to use the tools that could help our souls to grow, much like a child refusing to work the problems the teacher gives for learning math skills.

It is not necessary that we handle every crisis well; in fact we probably won't. We will make mistakes, but through them we will learn. The fifth time we have to deal with a sibling argument will be easier than the first. It doesn't matter if we fail. What matters is that we keep on trying. With regard to what we take with us to the after life, Leslie Weatherhead wrote, "Not what I have done, but what I have become through my doing seems of immense importance."[11]

Howard Thurman wrote similarly about using difficulties as tools for soul growth: "The spiritual life resembles a fertile egg whose embryo is surrounded by the exact sustenance needed for its development. It grows by feeding on its environment, achieving the strength needed finally to peck through the shell. So, likewise, the spiritual germ— 'the spark of the soul' within each human being—is surrounded by the exact food necessary for its development. This food consists of the essence of all the circumstances, the difficulties, the opportunities, the relationships—personal and universal—in which each person at every moment of time is environed. But [we] tend to resist, even to fight against this given sustenance. [We] fail to recognize it as the perfect nutrient for [our] spiritual and psychological development."[12]

> 3. *Can you see ways in which certain kinds of stress are helping your children grow into their potential? How about your own growth? How can you help everyone in your family use stress to enhance, not inhibit, growth?*

4. Being Stretched by Tension.

Another dictionary definition of *tension* is "the act of stretching or the condition of being stretched." What a parable this is for our lives! Every day as we respond to the challenge of being a parent, we are called to stretch beyond where we are. We think, for instance, that we have been as patient as a parent can be, that we have indeed reached our limit of patience, then a circumstance calls forth more patience than we have ever had to exercise before. We decide we have trusted our teenager as much as we can and then find that we have to extend this trust a bit more. We are asked to forgive again when we thought we had forgiven all we could.

The New Testament is full of unreachable ideals which challenge us to stretch again and again when we thought we could go no further. When Jesus said, "Turn the other cheek, go the second mile, forgive seventy times seven," he was giving us concepts for mature disciples, not for children in the faith or casual followers. If we have committed ourselves to follow Jesus, then the situations that cause us stress are also challenges to stretch our spiritual muscles by trying to apply these mature principles to the problems of parenting.

We may think we can't do this. We may think we have come to the end of our rope and that what we are being asked to do is not possible for us. I have felt this way a number of times, but I know from my own experiences and that of other committed religious persons that the seemingly impossible can be done with the help of God.

Recently I attended a meeting at which friends from many churches had gathered for a picnic and program. As I looked around I realized I was in the company of extraordinary individuals. I knew these people and something of what they had faced or were facing as parents. Here was a couple whose adult son suffered with schizophrenia, for which there is no known permanent cure; a year ago he had burned down their garage. Here was a couple whose daughter had tried several times to take her life. There were two young couples who had adopted children who had been abused, one a victim of repeated sexual abuse. There was a widow raising two girls, one of whom was in the throes of teenage rebellion. There was a family with a retarded son.

I thought of other parents in the churches we had served, people whose hearts had been so stretched by the circumstances life had given them and so filled with the love of God that they had been able to accept incredible things. There was the mother who loved without any condition her son who was a homosexual. There were families who lived through divorces of their adult children, continued to love the divorced in-laws, accepted new in-laws and their children from previous relationships. There were the grandparents whose daughter-in-law left their son and who took the grandchildren until their son remarried. There was the mother who took in the estranged wife of her son who had left him for another man and who returned seven-months pregnant, bruised and beaten by her present partner. "She had nowhere to go," this mother said. "How could I turn her away?"

All of those situations may sound like a soap opera, but they are the reality of our present age. These people to whom these circumstances were happening were not degenerate, irresponsible parents who brought this on themselves. They were committed Christians, moral, loving, concerned fathers and mothers. They did not "deserve" what had happened to them or their children.

Yet none of them were bitter. None of them were trying to hold themselves together with drugs or alcohol. Instead they were singing praises to God, discussing the problems of the world and what they could do to be part of the solution. They were stretching and growing and continually becoming new beings as they adjusted to the circumstances of our present age.

What is true for them can be true for us. We may or may not have to deal with what these parents have, but it is certain that we will be facing stress and crisis of some kind throughout our parenting. We can look upon this as bad news, complaining about what life and the evils of today's society have brought upon us. Or we can see it as the means by which we can grow into the likeness of the God of love who created and is continuing to create us. This is good news!

> 4. Like the author, bring to mind some Christians you know who have been stretched by times of difficulty and stress—who have not been destroyed but are growing, serving, and praising God. What is their secret?
>
> 5. In general, how can you come to accept stress as a challenge, as a "means by which you can grow into the likeness of the God of love"? How, for you, can stress become an opportunity for good news instead of bad?

NOTES

1. "The New American Family," *Ladies' Home Journal,* August, 1983, p. 167.
2. *The Book of Hymns* (Nashville: The Methodist Publishing House, 1966), no. 234.
3. Catherine Marshall, *Something More* (New York: Avon Books, 1976), p. 35.
4. William Barclay, *The Gospel of Matthew,* vol. 1, Revised Edition (Philadelphia: The Westminster Press, 1977), p. 258.
5. Leslie D. Weatherhead, *The Will of God* (Nashville: Abingdon Press, 1944), p. 11.
6. Ibid., p. 33.
7. Russell Baker, *Growing Up* (New York: New American Library, 1982), p. 61.
8. Howard Thurman, *Disciplines of the Spirit* (New York: Harper and Row, 1963), pp. 86-87.
9. Bruce C. Birch, "Biblical Faith and the Loss of Children," *The Christian Century,* October 26, 1983, p. 967.
10. Walt Schafer, *Stress, Distress and Growth* (Davis, California: Responsible Action, 1978), p. 18.
11. Leslie D. Weatherhead, *Life Begins at Death* (Nashville: Abingdon, 1969), p. 22.
12. *The Choice Is Always Ours,* edited by Dorothy B. Phillips, Elizabeth B. Howes, and Lucille M. Nixon (Wheaton, Illinois: The Theosophical Publishing House, 1982), p. 206.

THE BIBLE AND DIFFICULT RELATIONSHIPS

The Bible is a resource for handling difficult relationships. Here are some suggested passages for specific situations.

1. When you find it hard to forgive another or don't want to forgive — Matthew 6:12, 14 and Matthew 18:21-35

2. When you yourself need forgiveness — Psalm 103

3. When you know or sense that someone has something against you — Matthew 5:23-24

4. When someone has become your enemy and you are sure that God is on your side — Matthew 5:43-48

5. When you think that another person's behavior, lifestyle, ideas, etc., are wrong — Matthew 7:1-5 and James 4:11-12

6. When you are tempted to say something hurtful about another — James 3:3-12 and Ephesians 4:29-32

7. When someone says something hurtful to you or about you — 1 Peter 3:9-17

8. When someone does you a wrong — Romans 12:14-21

9. When you have grown discouraged over a difficult relationship — Isaiah 40:26-31

10. When you want to know what it means to love someone unconditionally — 1 Corinthians 13:4-7

RESOURCES

Parenting

A Very Practical Guide to Disciplining Young Children, Grace Mitchell, Telshore Publishing Company.
Between Parent and Child, Haim Ginott, Avon Books.
Child Behavior, Frances L. Ilg and Louise Bates Ames (Gisell Institute of Child Development), Harper and Brothers.
Christian Parenting for Peace and Justice, Kathleen and James McGinnis, Orbis Books.
Liberated Parents/Liberated Children, Adele Faber and Elaine Mazlish, Avon Books.
Self-Esteem: A Family Affair, Jean Illsley Clarke, Winston Press.
Family Survival (Coping with Stress), Parker Rossman, Pilgrim Press.

Divorce and/or Single Parenting

Helping Children of Divorce, Neal C. Buchanan and Eugene Chamberlain, Broadman Press.
Father and Son, Darrell Sifford, Bridgebooks.
I Didn't Plan to Be a Single Parent, Bobbie Reed, Concordia.
Suddenly Single, Jim Smoke, Revell Company.
The Single Parent, Virginia Watts Smith, Revell Company.
Talking about Divorce and Separation, Earl A. Gallman, Beacon Press.
From Separation to Connection: A Guide to Communication . . . for Parents of Divorce and Their Children (a booklet and audio cassette), Sam Frowine, Creative Connections, Inc., P.O. Box 2768, Morganton, NC 28655.

Remarriage and Stepparenting

Help for Remarried Couples and Families, Richard Olson and Carole Della Pia-Terry, Judson Press.
Ministry with Remarried Persons, Olson and Pia-Terry, Judson Press.

Death

Helping Children with the Mystery of Death, Elizabeth Reed, Abingdon.
Life Begins at Death, Leslie D. Weatherhead, Abingdon.
The Fall of Freddie the Leaf, Leo Buscaglia, Holt, Rinehart, and Winston.
When Bad Things Happen to Good People, Harold S. Kushner, Avon Books.